# CONDITION OF ACCESS

# CONDITION OF ACCESS

## Higher Education
### for Lower Income Students

**Edited by Donald E. Heller**

**Foreword by Juliet V. Garcia**

AMERICAN COUNCIL ON EDUCATION
PRAEGER
Series on Higher Education

**Library of Congress Cataloging-in-Publication Data**

Condition of access : higher education for lower income students / edited by Donald E. Heller ; foreword by Juliet V. Garcia.
     p. cm. — (American Council on Education/ Praeger series on higher education)
Includes bibliographical references and index.
  ISBN 1–57356–517–2 (alk. paper)
  1. Youth with social disabilities—Education (Higher)—United States.
2. Student aid—United States.  I. Heller, Donald E.  II. Series.
  LC4069.6 .C66 2002
  378.1'9826'9420973—dc21  2002070351

Formerly ACE/Oryx Press Series on Higher Education

British Library Cataloguing in Publication Data is available.

Copyright © 2002 by American Council on Education and Praeger Publishers

Library of Congress Catalog Card Number: 2002070351
ISBN: 1–57356–517–2

First published in 2002

Praeger Publishers, 88 Post Road West, Westport, CT 06881
An imprint of Greenwood Publishing Group, Inc.
www.praeger.com

Printed in the United States of America

The paper used in this book complies with the
Permanent Paper Standard issued by the National
Information Standards Organization (Z39.48–1984).

P

# Contents

# Foreword

O ur nation stands at a critical juncture, one that will determine our economic future for a significant portion of this century and the educational opportunity available to many Americans. Currently, increasing numbers of lower-income students graduate from high school academically prepared to enter college, but they confront significant financial barriers that prevent enrollment and persistence. In addition, demographic forces already at work will ensure a dramatic increase in the number of 18- to 24-year-olds enrolled in college—1.6 million more by 2015. A disproportionate number of these students will be from lower-income families, and a greater percentage of this generation will be well prepared for college.

Yet, at a time in which higher education has never been more important to the economy, nor the economic returns to its citizens any greater, the current generation of lower-income youth lack access to a college education. And the serious access problem we face today could easily develop into an access crisis for the next generation if not addressed effectively. Averting this crisis will require reasserting access to college and the opportunity to pursue a bachelor's degree as a national priority and reinstating the nation's access goal—an implicit promise to lower-income families. That goal and promise has always been to ensure, at a minimum, that lower-income students have the opportunity to attend either a two-year or four-year public institution full-time and not be constrained unduly by high costs that are unmet by financial aid and, accordingly, the necessity to work or borrow excessively.

This book brings together skilled researchers to discuss the current state of access for lower-income students to America's institutions of higher education. It results from a series of papers commissioned by the Advisory Committee on Student Financial Assistance, an independent source of advice and counsel to Congress and the Secretary of Education on student financial aid policy. Each scholar submitted a chapter to build a research base for understanding the access problem that faces our nation. The most recent research available on the state of college access for lower-income students can be found in this volume.

The Advisory Committee not only commissioned these papers but also conducted a series of meetings and developed a policy perspective on the state of access. The Advisory Committee held a sequence of three inter-related public meetings devoted to the committee's most important legislative charge: improving postsecondary access for lower-income students. The first meeting was held at the University of Mississippi in April 1999, the second meeting at Boston University in April 2000, and the concluding meeting at the University of Vermont in September 2000. The findings from each meeting served to further define and identify an effective long-run federal strategy to improve access.

In February 2001, the Advisory Committee released a companion report to this book that focuses on the policy implications of the research presented by the authors of this volume. This report, entitled *Access Denied: Restoring the Nation's Commitment to Equal Educational Opportunity*, is designed to bring access back to the forefront of federal higher education and student aid policy. The most compelling finding of this report is that no matter how dramatically academic preparation advances, without significant increases in financial aid, college participation and completion gaps between the rich and the poor will widen, increasing economic and social stratification in the nation.

The chapters contained in this volume, then, are about access to post-secondary education for lower-income students—middle-school students who are now preparing for college, as we have insisted that they do; high school students contemplating the feasibility of attending college; and college students struggling to persist to degree. The researchers who have contributed to this book look at the price signals lower-income students are receiving, the educational behaviors those price signals are causing, and the consequences for both them and the nation if we fail to maintain our commitment to access to higher education for all.

*Juliet V. Garcia*

# Preface

E arly in George W. Bush's presidency, the Advisory Committee on Student Financial Assistance issued a report entitled *Access Denied: Restoring the Nation's Commitment to Equal Educational Opportunity* (2001). That report laid out a compelling argument for reaffirming our nation's commitment to providing financial aid and other forms of support for the country's neediest students. *Condition of Access: Higher Education for Lower Income Students* builds on the committee's earlier work by examining in detail the challenges faced by policymakers, higher education institutions, students and their families, and others in meeting this commitment.[1]

The United States has recently enjoyed a period of prosperity that has bestowed unprecedented wealth on the nation and many American families. Yet at the same time, this prosperity has done little to move the country toward the ideals articulated over half a century ago by President Harry Truman's Commission on Higher Education:

> It is the responsibility of the community, at the local, State, and National levels, to guarantee that financial barriers do not prevent any able and otherwise qualified young person from receiving the opportunity for higher education. There must be developed in this country the widespread realization that money expended for education is the wisest and soundest of investments in the national interest. The democratic community cannot tolerate a society based upon education for the well-to-do alone. If college opportunities are restricted to those in the higher income brackets, the way is open to the creation and perpetuation of a class society which has no place in the American way of life. (President's Commission on Higher Education, 1947, Vol. 2, p. 23)

This book shows how shifts in educational policy at the federal, state, and institutional levels have affected access to higher education for students of different backgrounds. Most important, the book projects the impact of current policies on the large cohort of college-age students that will surge out of American high schools over the next twenty years. The coming period will challenge our country to produce the highly skilled workforce needed for the twenty-first century, as well as to productively absorb an increasing immigrant population and attack the causes of poverty.

The first section examines the postsecondary education participation patterns of lower-income students in the nation.[2] Brian K. Fitzgerald and Jennifer A. Delaney of the Advisory Committee provide an historical analysis of the efforts to promote educational opportunity in the United States. They also provide a context for the current status of lower-income students in higher education today.

In Chapter 2, John B. Lee of JBL Associates, Inc., compares the characteristics of students who differ in levels of expected family contribution (EFC) to college costs. A number of factors determine a student's EFC as measured by higher education institutions, including family income, assets, number of children in the family attending college, and the cost of the institution attended. However, in general, the more available student and family resources, the larger the EFC. Using EFC as a measure, Lee demonstrates how the emphasis in financial aid programs has changed in recent years.

The second section of the book analyzes the status of student financial aid programs provided by three primary sources in the United States: the federal government, state governments, and higher education institutions themselves. In Chapter 3, Lawrence E. Gladieux, an education policy analyst, looks at trends in federal assistance provided for college financing to students and their families. He illustrates how the focus of federal support for students has shifted away from the original goals of the Higher Education Act of 1965, which include ensuring access to higher education for low-income students. Instead, changing the mix of grant and loan programs has increased the affordability of college for middle- and upper-income students.

I examine the support provided by state governments in Chapter 4. States subsidize the price of higher education through direct appropriations to institutions, which tend to keep tuitions low, and through targeted forms of financial aid, which have traditionally aided low-income students. In that chapter I describe how many states have shifted the burden of financing the cost of college from the public to students and their families, and how financial aid for college is being used more frequently to reward academic achievement, rather than help accomplish the goal of equality of educational opportunity.

Michael S. McPherson of Macalester College and Morton Owen Schapiro of Williams College are both college presidents and long-time researchers of the economics of higher education. In Chapter 5 they analyze student financial assistance provided directly by colleges and universities to undergraduates. They document how institutional aid has changed from a resource for needy students to a merit award serving as an enrollment management tool. They also analyze the interrelated nature of institutionally based and federal financial aid, including college tax credit programs.

Providing financial assistance for college is not enough to ensure that lower-income students attend and succeed in a college or university. Academic and social factors also play a role in preparation for and persistence in higher education. In the third section of the book, two chapters look at efforts designed to supplement the student financial assistance programs. In Chapter 6 Laura W. Perna of the University of Maryland and Watson Scott Swail examine early intervention programs, such as the federally funded TRIO and GEARUP efforts. These programs try to reach students as early as middle school to help boost their academic preparation for college, as well as socialize them to the importance of attaining a college degree. Once in college, many lower-income students require assistance in the form of social and academic support. David W. Breneman of the University of Virginia and Jamie P. Merisotis of the Institute for Higher Education Policy look at the efforts to provide remedial instruction and other forms of support to underprepared students in Chapter 7.

Having considered the current state of access to and preparation for college by lower-income students, the book next turns toward the future. Anthony P. Carnevale and Richard A. Fry of the Educational Testing Service in Chapter 8 examine the demographic trends facing the nation over the next fifteen years, focusing on the likely increased demand for college and the subsequent implications for student financial aid policy. In Chapter 9, A. Clayton Spencer of Harvard University examines the current political context in which higher education finds itself and provides recommendations for moving the country toward the ideals articulated by the Truman Commission over half a century ago.

This book, following on the heels of *Access Denied*, documents the growing gap in college participation between rich and poor in our nation. Our findings are presented as a stimulus to discussion of the barriers to postsecondary education facing the country's neediest students. We hope the book will point the way toward a reevaluation and restructuring of our nation's policies to better achieve equity in access to postsecondary education for all Americans, regardless of their economic status.

*Donald E. Heller*

## NOTES

1. The focus of this book is on access to baccalaureate education in the United States.

2. Throughout the report, the authors have used different definitions of " lower-income students." This is primarily the result of different measures in the variety of data sets available for analyzing the status of postsecondary participation in the United States. In each chapter the authors provide the specific definition of income categories that they use.

## REFERENCES

Advisory Committee on Student Financial Assistance. (2001). *Access denied: Restoring the nation's commitment to equal educational opportunity.* Washington, DC: Advisory Committee on Student Financial Assistance.

President's Commission on Higher Education. (1947). *Higher education for American democracy,* Vol. 2. New York: Harper & Brothers.

# Acknowledgments

In the spring of 2000, I was approached by Brian Fitzgerald, staff director of the Advisory Committee on Student Financial Assistance, about the possibility of editing a report on the issues related to lower-income students in higher education. I had recently met Brian and had been invited to address the Advisory Committee at its April 2000 meeting in Boston. My initial reaction was to decline a leadership role in the report, because of other commitments I had at the time, and instead offer to be one of the contributors.

After meeting with Brian and his staff, however, I was persuaded that the proposed project was both interesting and immensely important to the future of higher education policy in the country. The nation would shortly have a new administration in Washington, and the Advisory Committee wanted to play an active role in helping to shape the policy debate that would inevitably result. Brian promised the full support of and resources from the Advisory Committee in completing the project, a promise that he helped fulfill.

The first wise move the Advisory Committee made was to bring together an outstanding group of authors to examine the key issues facing lower-income students in higher education. The initial work of these authors was partially reflected in *Access Denied: Restoring the Nation's Commitment to Equal Educational Opportunity*, the Advisory Committee's report issued in February 2001. The issuance of the report was followed by a symposium held at the Harvard Graduate School of Education in March 2001, where many of the contributors to *Access Denied* discussed their findings with an audience of educators, policymakers, and researchers.

*Condition of Access: Higher Education for Lower Income Students* brings together many of the authors who initially worked with the Advisory Committee, and others who joined the effort to contribute to this book. The volume could not have been completed without the efforts of the chapter authors, and I thank each of them for their dedicated and committed efforts on a project that came together very quickly. William Goggin of the Advisory Committee read and provided his thoughts on many of the initial papers. Perry Frank provided editorial assistance on many of the initial papers submitted to the Advisory Committee. Editorial assistance was also provided by Betty Pessagno of Greenwood Publishing Group. James Murray and Jacqueline King of the American Council on Education provided support for the book to be published as part of the ACE/Praeger Series on Higher Education.

Brian Fitzgerald and Jennifer Delaney of the Advisory Committee played a crucial role in the creation of this volume. In addition to contributing their own chapter, they acted as liaisons with many of the paper contributors and assisted in the initial review of many of the chapters. Their feedback and insights were critical to the shaping of this book, and I could not have completed the project without their assistance.

My former colleagues at the University of Michigan, though not directly involved in the project, were encouraging of my work on it. My colleagues at the Pennsylvania State University have expressed their support of and interest in my work on the topic of educational opportunity.

Finally, I wish to express my gratitude to my wife, Anne Simon, for her support of my research on postsecondary educational opportunity. This book was one more project that I did not have to take on, yet she encouraged me to pursue it and dedicate my efforts to it. For this, among other things, I thank her.

# Contributors

**David W. Breneman** currently serves as dean of the Curry School of Education at the University of Virginia. In addition to his publications on higher education finance, liberal arts colleges, and public policy, he is executive editor of *Change* magazine. Previously Dr. Breneman was a visiting professor at the Harvard Graduate School of Education, president of Kalamazoo College, and a Senior Fellow in the economic studies program at Brookings. Dr. Breneman earned a B.A. in philosophy from the University of Colorado and a Ph.D. in economics from the University of California, Berkeley.

**Anthony P. Carnevale** is vice president for public leadership at the Educational Testing Service. He has also served as a presidentially appointed chair of the National Commission for Employment Policy; vice president and director of the Human Resource Studies at the Committee for Economic Development; and president of the Institute for Workbased Learning, an applied research center affiliated with the American Society for Training and Development. He received his B.A. from Colby College and his Ph.D. from the Maxwell School at Syracuse University.

**Jennifer A. Delaney** is the former assistant staff director for research at the Advisory Committee on Student Financial Assistance. In 2000, she earned a Master of Education degree with a concentration in higher education from the Harvard Graduate School of Education. She received a Bachelor of Arts degree in English from the University of Michigan in 1999.

**Brian K. Fitzgerald** has served as staff director of the Advisory Committee on Student Financial Assistance since March 1988. He also serves as adjunct associate professor of public policy at American University in Washington, D.C., where he teaches courses in the politics of public policy and education. For many years he has been involved in policy development and in research and redesign of student aid programs when he worked at Pelavin Associates, Inc., and Advanced Technology, Inc. He received his Ed.D. in policy research and his Ed.M., with a concentration in higher education policy and administration, from the Harvard Graduate School of Education. He received his B.A. in literature from the Massachusetts College of Liberal Arts.

**Richard A. Fry** is senior economist at the Educational Testing Service. He specializes as a demographic economist with expertise in the empirical analysis of U.S. labor markets and higher education. He is an active member of the American Economics Association, the Society of Labor Economists, and the Population Association of America. His work has been published in numerous professional journals, including *Industrial Relations, Contemporary Economic Policy,* the *Quarterly Review of Economics and Finance,* and *Population Research and Policy Review.* He received his Ph.D. in economics from the University of Michigan and his B.A. from Calvin College in Grand Rapids, Michigan.

**Juliet V. Garcia** is chair of the Advisory Committee on Student Financial Assistance. Since 1992, she has been the president of the University of Texas at Brownsville in partnership with Texas Southmost College. Prior to her current position, she served as dean of arts and sciences. She is a board member of the White House Initiative on Educational Excellence for Hispanic Americans, the Ford Foundation's Campus Diversity Initiative, and the Carnegie Foundation for the Advancement of Teaching. Dr. Garcia received her B.A. and M.A. degrees in Speech and English from the University of Houston, and her Ph.D. in Communications and Linguistics from the University of Texas at Austin.

**Lawrence E. Gladieux** is a consultant on education and public policy living in Potomac Falls, Virginia. His clients have included the Century Foundation, EdFund of California, the James Irvine Foundation, the Federal Advisory Committee on Student Financial Assistance, the National Center for Public Policy and Higher Education, the College Board, and the U.S. Department of Education. From 1981 to 1993 he was executive director of the Washington office of the College Board, and from 1993 to 2000 he was the organization's executive director for policy analysis. He has presented testimony to Congress and written widely on issues of the high school-to-college transition, equity, access, affordability, and the impact of technology on the delivery of higher education. He received his bachelor's degree cum laude in government from Oberlin College, where he now serves as a trustee, and he received his master's from the Woodrow Wilson School of Public and International Affairs at Princeton University.

**Donald E. Heller** is associate professor and senior research associate in the Center for the Study of Higher Education at the Pennsylvania State University College of Education. Prior to his current appointment, he was an assistant professor of education at the University of Michigan. He teaches and conducts research on issues related to higher education economics, public policy, and finance. He is the editor of the book *The States and Public Higher Education Policy: Affordability, Access, and Accountability* (Johns Hopkins University Press, 2001). He received his Ed.D. in higher education and Ed.M. in administration, planning, and social policy from the Harvard Graduate School of Education and his B.A. in economics and political science from Tufts University.

**John B. Lee** is currently the president of JBL Associates, Inc., an independent consulting firm that specializes in postsecondary education policy analysis. Previously, Dr. Lee worked for Abt Associates, the Education and Labor Committee of the U.S. House of Representatives, the Education Commission of the States, and Stanford Research International. He also spent time as an instructor, academic senate president, and president of the faculty union at Laney Community College in Oakland, California. He holds a B.A. and M.A. from California State University at Sacramento and an Ed.D. in postsecondary administration from the University of California at Berkeley.

**Michael S. McPherson** is president of Macalester College. In addition to being an author of many articles and books dealing with the topic of higher education and economics, he is a trustee of the College Board in New York, a trustee of the Minneapolis Institute of Arts, and a member of the Board of Senior Scholars of the National Center for Postsecondary Improvement at Stanford University. Previously he served as a senior fellow in economic studies at the Brookings Institute and a fellow at the Institute for Advanced Study at Princeton. At Williams College, he held the titles of professor, chair of the economics department, and dean of the faculty. He received his B.A., M.A., and Ph.D. degrees from the University of Chicago.

**Jamie P. Merisotis** is founder and president of the Institute for Higher Education Policy, a nonprofit, nonpartisan organization that espouses a mission to foster access to and quality in postsecondary education. He is a recognized expert on higher education financing, student demographics and outcomes, minority-serving colleges and universities, technology-based learning, and federal policy development. Previously, he served as executive director of the bipartisan National Commission on Responsibilities for Financing Postsecondary Education.

**Laura W. Perna** is assistant professor in the department of education policy and leadership at the University of Maryland. Her research uses an integrated theoretical approach to identify the ways in which social structures limit the ability of women, racial and ethnic minorities, and individuals of lower socioeconomic status to realize the economic, social, and political opportunities associated with two aspects of higher education: access as a student and employment as a faculty member. She holds a Ph.D. in higher education and an M.P.P. in public policy from the University of Michigan and a B.A. in psychology and a B.S. in economics from the University of Pennsylvania.

**Morton Owen Schapiro** is president of Williams College. He also serves on the board of the journal *Educational Economics* and is co-editor of the Economics of Education book series through the University of Michigan Press. He is an authority on college financing, affordability, education costs, and student aid. Previously he held the position of dean of the University of Southern California's College of Letters, Arts and Sciences and was professor of economics at Williams College. Dr. Schapiro received a bachelor's degree in economics from Hofstra University, and master's and doctorate degrees in economics from the University of Pennsylvania.

**A. Clayton Spencer** is associate vice president for higher education policy at Harvard University. Prior to this position, she served as Chief Education Counsel for the U.S. Senate Committee on Labor and Human Resources, from June 1993 until January 1997, and has also served as an associate in the law firm of Ropes and Gray. Previously, she practiced as an assistant U.S. attorney in Boston. She holds a B.A. from Williams College, master's degrees from Oxford University and Harvard University, and a J.D. from Yale Law School.

**Watson Scott Swail** is director of The Pell Institute for the Study of Opportunity in Higher Education, a research center sponsored by The Council for Opportunity in Education. Research at The Pell Institute focuses on the educational opportunity of low-income, underrepresented students, including precollege outreach programs, student financial aid, college persistence, and distance education. Dr. Swail directed and authored the College Board's *Outreach Program Handbook 2001*, released in September 2000,

and chaired the ConnectED 2000 National Summit on College Preparation and Opportunity. Recent articles include "Preparing America's Disadvantaged for College: Programs That Increase College Opportunity"
(*New Directions for Institutional Research* series) and "Beyond Access: Increasing the Odds of College Success" (*Phi Delta Kappan*). In addition to
his research and writing, Dr. Swail teaches educational policy and research
at The George Washington University, where he received his doctorate in
educational policy.

# PART I

## College Access Issues for Lower Income Students

# CHAPTER 1

# Educational Opportunity in America

*Brian K. Fitzgerald and Jennifer A. Delaney*

At the dawn of the twenty-first century, higher education is more important than ever before. Intrinsically linked to the importance of higher education is the ideal that all Americans, regardless of family income, should have the opportunity for access to postsecondary education. Unfortunately, as history has shown, this ideal is not easily achieved. Despite the creation of a series of federal programs designed to address the issue of access, today's college students, particularly lower-income[1] college students, face enormous challenges in achieving access to higher education. Impending demographic growth and rising college costs pose serious policy dilemmas for federal and state policymakers to a degree not seen since the 1960s. This demographic growth will dramatically increase the number of students on America's campuses. Equally as important to higher education and policymakers, 80 percent of this group will be non-white, almost half will be Hispanic (see Chapter 8), and a disproportionate number will be low- and moderate-income—those most likely to be eligible for student financial aid. The demographic pressures will be exacerbated by college costs, which have risen faster than inflation, with the highest rates of growth occurring at public institutions that enroll 80 percent of all undergraduate students.

The twin forces of demographic growth and rising college costs will place strains on federal and state policymaking and institutional decision-making processes. The growth in the number of needy students and college costs will substantially increase the demand for federal student aid funds, currently in excess of $50 billion (College Board, 2001b), and pose serious challenges to the national commitment of providing access to higher education for low- and moderate-income families. The manner and depth of responses by federal and state policymakers and institutional decisionmakers will determine the level of access to higher education enjoyed by the next generation of Americans.[2]

Ironically, today's challenges bear a striking resemblance to those faced nearly forty years ago when the nation's first comprehensive commitment to access to higher education was articulated in the Higher Education Act of 1965. This legislation was propelled by concerns that are virtually identical to the challenges that face our nation today: swelling enrollments, inadequate capacity on college campuses, and the recognition that financial barriers severely restrict the access to higher education.[3] The debate over higher education, which shaped the contemporary federal role in higher education and the programs that support access today, is, in many ways, as old as the nation itself. By reviewing the history and effectiveness of the federal role in higher education, this chapter seeks to analyze today's access challenges.

## HISTORY OF THE FEDERAL ROLE IN HIGHER EDUCATION

From the founding of the Republic, Americans have instinctively known the importance of higher education to the nation and its citizens. Delegates to the Constitutional Convention in 1787 debated the creation of a national university that would have established an "educational federalism" to mirror the relationship of the federal government with states and localities (Hofstadter & Smith, 1961; Rainsford, 1972; Ellis, 2001). Conventional delegates rejected a national university and our Constitution as ratified makes no mention of higher education. Nevertheless, at key points in each of the three previous centuries, the nation harnessed higher education for economic growth and the social good of the nation. In one of its earliest acts, Congress enacted the Northwest Ordinance in 1787, which provided land grants to fund institutions of higher education (Rainsford, 1972). As westward expansion continued, Congress broadened the practice of providing resources to higher education through land grants, in the first Morrill Act of 1862. This act, and the subsequent Morrill Act in 1890, gave rise to a system of public universities in each state to ensure agricultural and economic development (Rivlin, 1961). Reflecting the social aspirations of the nation, Horace Mann recognized the power of education, asserting that education "beyond all other devices of human origin, is the great equalizer of the conditions of men" (Mann, 1867).

At the close of World War II, the modern federal role emerged as higher education was called upon to reintegrate America's veterans into a peacetime society, propel the economy from a dark period of recession and war, and assist in fighting the Cold War. The Servicemen's Readjustment Act of 1944, known as the GI Bill, provided educational benefits to 3.5 million veterans by 1960, ensuring a smooth integration of veterans into the postwar economy and contributing to a postwar economic boom (Rivlin, 1961). The GI Bill provided unprecedented educational opportunity to a generation of Americans. It also provided an important model for future federal interventions: The administration of the GI Bill moved funds for education directly into the hands of students (Rivlin, 1970). In 1947, the Truman Commission further outlined the modern federal purpose and role by calling for democratizing higher education through the elimination of financial barriers that caused underparticipation in higher education by low- and moderate-income Americans (President's Commission on Higher Education, 1947).

Our nation again called upon higher education in response to Soviet superiority in space. Shocked by the launch of Sputnik, Congress linked education to national defense in the passage of the National Defense Education Act (NDEA) in 1958 (Sundquist, 1968). The federal justification for aiding college students with loans was to increase the supply of educated persons to fulfill the country's new demand for enhanced national defense (Wolanin, 2001). The act fundamentally altered and expanded the federal role in supplementing states in funding higher education and set the stage for the creation of the most significant federal role in higher education: broad-based student financial assistance (Gladieux & Wolanin, 1976).

In the 1960s, the nation faced a different kind of crisis—a crisis of opportunity and equity. Census data from the late 1960s indicate that students from high-income families were five times more likely to attend college than students from lower-income families (Gladieux & Wolanin, 1976). Race and ethnicity also played a substantial role in determining college attendance. Minorities were significantly underrepresented in four-year institutions and were overrepresented at less selective institutions, a pattern that could not be explained by variations in ability (Gladieux & Wolanin, 1976).

In response to the opportunity crisis, the nation promised lower-income youth that they would no longer face financial barriers to higher education that exceeded those of their middle- and upper-income peers, as expressed in the passage of the Higher Education Act of 1965. The rationale for creating the 1965 act was articulated by two distinct policy justifications—

economic opportunity and social equity. Policymakers focused on economic opportunity because the invisible hand of a capitalist market would not provide adequate opportunities for individuals to attend college. Accordingly, society was unable to benefit fully from the positive externalities of postsecondary education: a more flexible workforce, a more informed citizenry, a lower crime rate, a higher regard for the environment, a higher level of public health, and overall increased economic productivity.

Likewise, the social equity justification for federal financial aid was enticing to policymakers because of its focus on providing all citizens with equal opportunities for personal advancement through participation in higher education (Wolanin, 2001).[4] Large wage differentials, which are often used as a proxy for measuring personal advancement, were evident during the 1960s and served as a driving argument for the social equity justification of financial aid. Even today, the importance of higher education for individual advancement is striking. For example, in 1999 earning a bachelor's degree raised median annual household income by 75 percent over holding only a high school diploma—from $35,744 to $64,406 (Figure 1.1).

Given society's desire to capture the positive externalities of higher education and to promote social equity, the federal financial aid system was carefully crafted to fit into preexisting notions of educational policy. A fundamental principle of American democracy was that education, and in this case higher education, was primarily the responsibility of the states or local governments, not the federal government. By limiting its distribution of funds to institutions in the support of research and to students through federal financial aid, the federal government was able to support higher education while preserving the authority and autonomy of the states.[5] Its purpose was to grant access by equalizing educational opportunity among students from differing socioeconomic circumstances.

In making the promise of access, the long-term policy goal of the 1965 act was clear: to narrow over time the unacceptable income-related gaps existing in postsecondary participation, persistence, and degree completion. The consideration of the bill in the U.S. House of Representatives and Senate also showed that congressmen and senators were painfully aware that the impending explosion in enrollments, caused by the baby boom generation, would tax the capacity of institutions of higher education. Therefore, the opportunity of many in this generation to attend college would be limited by financial barriers (Congressional Record, 1965). The 1965 act reflected these concerns by creating programs designed to assist institutions in building capacity and, more importantly, in creating a new set of policy instruments to address inequality of educational opportunity.

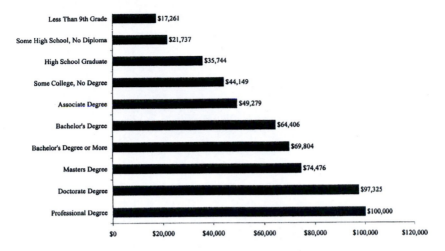

*Figure 1.1  Median Annual Household Income, by Educational Attainment of Householder, 1999*

Source: College Board (2001a).

To combat unequal opportunities, the policy instrument of choice was need-based student aid, which directed aid toward those students whose families could not be reasonably expected to contribute to higher education expenses as a result of low levels of income. For the first time, the federal government provided need-based grants, Educational Opportunity Grants, to students of "exceptional need," by providing funds to institutions. These grants and other forms of aid, including work-study and federally guaranteed loans, would subsidize the cost of attending postsecondary education after taking into account a fair assessment of the family's own ability to pay for college. Policymakers understood that it was necessary to minimize the residual expenses of postsecondary education not covered by the family contribution or student aid, now referred to as unmet need, because such costs were known to be central to family decisions about what type of postsecondary education students could attend.

Policymakers also had no doubt that lower-income families, when faced with excessive unmet need, were exhibiting a stream of counterproductive educational choices, despite the high rate of return to postsecondary education. The 1965 act also focused on ensuring that students were aware of college opportunity and adequately prepared for higher education by creating the Upward Bound and Talent Search programs. Additionally, it created the Student Support program to aid students in persisting to degree completion. Eliminating financial barriers and enhancing preparation and persistence were seen as essential investments, good for both youth and society.

The Higher Education Act of 1965 and the Education Amendments of 1972, which reauthorized the 1965 act, represented watersheds in federal policy from two important perspectives. First, Congress rejected calls for increased aid to institutions and embraced the notion that the most effective means of achieving equal opportunity was to provide funds directly to students, reflecting the structure and focus of the GI Bill (Rivlin, 1970). Consequently, the new Basic Educational Opportunity Grants (BEOG, later renamed and referred to as the Pell Grant program) were provided in the form of vouchers students could take to any eligible institution, ensuring student choice among institutions (Gladieux & Wolanin, 1976). Therefore the federal financial assistance programs provide aid that is both campus-based and portable. In addition, for the first time the federal government created entitlements for students.[6] The 1972 amendments also created a federal–state partnership to support the creation and expansion of state need-based grant programs, the State Student Incentive Grant program, recently renamed the Leveraging Educational Assistance Program. Regardless of the delivery method, direct to students or through states and institutions, the goal was the same: to increase access and equalize opportunity.

In order to narrow the gaps in postsecondary participation, persistence, and degree completion, the programs under the 1965 act and the 1972 amendments were designed to ensure, at a minimum, that the decision of lower-income students to attend either a two-year or a four-year public institution full time would not be unduly constrained by high unmet need and the consequent necessity to work or to borrow excessively. Indeed, the initial commitment was actually somewhat broader, that the programs, especially the Pell Grant program, would not only guarantee lower-income students access to public institutions but also provide a modest level of choice between public and private institutions. The Pell Grant program would provide this choice by the voucher, which would follow the student, as well as by the amount of the maximum grant, which by academic year 1975–1976 reached over 80 percent of the average cost of attendance at a four-year public institution and nearly 40 percent at private institutions (see Chapter 3).

The history of the federal role in higher education has always shown concern for access. Through the initial development of federal financial aid programs in the Truman Commission to the Higher Education Act of 1965, the focus of federal higher education policy–makers has been to promote access as a way of capturing the positive externalities of higher education and promoting social equity. Having examined the historical development of the federal financial aid programs, this chapter next considers how well the programs, created to address these issues of access, accomplish their objectives.

# EVALUATION OF FEDERAL HIGHER EDUCATION POLICY

The past thirty years have tested the federal financial aid programs and their impact on providing access. By looking at the federal financial aid system, researchers have been able to measure the effectiveness of these programs. Often researchers use the concept of an educational pipeline to think about access. Taken together, each step of the pipeline represents a sequential process through which students must pass to gain access to higher education. The pipeline involves steps such as gaining information about college, clarifying eighth-grade expectations, taking appropriate courses in high school, making college plans in twelfth grade, taking entrance exams, applying to college, enrolling in college, and persisting and graduating from college. This section considers the education pipeline that leads to college by focusing on factors that influence the decision to enroll in college and those that relate to persistence once a student enters an institution.[7] The goal of the following review of the research is to gauge advances in access that are attributable to the federal student aid programs.

Consequently, the research presented here concentrates primarily on the financial dimensions of access, while recognizing the importance of non-financial factors in the college access process. With a history as rich as the legacy of the financial aid programs, researchers have spent decades creating a large body of work that analyzes the effects of non-financial factors, like social and academic experiences, that are critical to student success.[8] In fact, even researchers who focus on financial factors often control or account for academic preparation by limiting their analysis to students who are enrolled in college. Likewise, implicit in our analysis of the impact of federal financial aid programs is an understanding that financial programs can be effective only if they are coupled with academic progress. Financial aid is a necessary, but not sufficient condition for promoting access to higher education. However, this section focuses on research regarding the financial components of access because these are the primary components of federal higher education legislation.

## Enrollment Effects

A substantial number of authors have examined an underlying assumption of the financial aid system, namely, that students place significant emphasis on their ability to finance their education in their decisions about postsecondary education (Jackson, 1978; Manski & Wise, 1983; St. John, 1994a, 1994b; Terenzini, Cabrera, & Bernal, 2001). The enrollment effects of federal financial aid programs can be traced through various steps in the education pipeline. As early as eighth grade, enrollment effects can be seen in the expectations that students hold for enrolling in college. Likewise, enrollment effects of federal financial aid programs are evident in high school seniors' plans for college, admissions test taking, college application submissions, and, ultimately enrollment in college.

One early effect of student financial aid is that it impacts the perceptions of students and their ability to imagine themselves attending college. Indeed, all the steps in the education pipeline that lead up to an official enrollment decision (e.g., expectations, plans, test taking, and applying) are influenced by financial aid. In her research, King (1996) discovered that lower-income students who expected to receive financial aid were more likely to aspire to college than were lower-income students who did not expect aid. Additionally, knowledge about financial aid can increase the number of higher education options a student considers. Flint (1992) showed that knowledge of financial aid allowed families to consider a wider range of institutions and influenced their financial planning. In sum, the perception of the availability of financial aid encourages thoughts of matriculation for students, particularly those from lower-income families (Choy & Ottinger, 1998; Hossler, Schmit, & Vesper, 1999; Jackson, 1978; King, 1996; Olson & Rosenfeld, 1984; St. John, 1994a, 1994b; St. John, Paulsen, & Starkey, 1996; Terenzini, Cabrera, & Bernal, 2001). These researchers concluded that the simple presence of financial aid, and the success stories that follow, is enough to encourage students to prepare for college and to take the steps necessary to enroll in an institution.

A student's reliance on financial aid varies in direct proportion to family income, however, with lower-income families relying on financial aid the most (Miller 1997). The U.S. Department of Education (1997) found that of all income levels of students, the lowest-socioeconomic students reported being much more concerned about financing their education when choosing a school. Tierney (1980) and Leslie, Johnson, and Carlson (1977) also indicated that the probability of a lower-income student attending college could be influenced by the perception that financial aid was available. For students enrolled in middle school and high school, financial aid is extremely important to enable lower-income students to actualize the goal of achieving access to higher education. Tierney (1980) echoed the findings of Leslie, Johnson, and Carlson (1977) by showing that higher-socioeconomic-status (higher-SES) students have greater access to information sources about financial aid than do the lowest-SES students. Since financial aid makes college seem possible, knowledge of it causes student to engage in the behaviors necessary for college matriculation, such as taking college preparatory courses, completing college admissions tests, and enrolling in early intervention programs.

In addition to the indirect effects of aid on the earlier stages of the pipeline, one of the most visible effects of student aid programs is that they increase overall, measurable, enrollment decisions. Over time studies have shown that lower-income students are especially price responsive. Even though researchers have disagreed about the correct models or measurements to be used, they all have shown a positive correlation between student financial aid and enrollment. Jackson (1978), for example, found increases in financial aid lead to an increase of students enrolling in college. Likewise the research community has shown that enrollments decrease as tuition increases. Consider, for instance, McPherson and Shapiro's (1998) estimation that increases in tuition would reduce enrollments.[9] Financial aid also counters the negative impact that tuition increases have on students. The negative impact of one dollar of tuition increase is neutralized by the positive effect of one dollar of grant aid (Manski & Wise, 1983). In particular, financial aid had a significant impact on lower-income students, since this type of student is more likely to respond to aid than are students from other income levels (Jackson, 1978; Manski & Wise, 1983). In their research on the Pell Grant program, Manski and Wise (1983) showed that the program was successful in encouraging enrollment in college for lower-income high school graduates. Likewise, financial aid can affect the choices that lower-income students have. The lowest-SES students at four-year public institutions were three times more likely than the highest-SES students (74 versus 28 percent) to claim that financial aid is very important in their choice of institution (Terenzini, Cabrera, & Bernal, 2001).

These findings suggest that financial aid is most effective for lower-income students because they are highly responsive to prices and would have lower probabilities of enrolling in college in the absence of financial aid (Jackson, 1978). From perceptions of financial aid in eighth grade to enrollment decisions following high school graduation, financial aid has a positive impact on the enrollment steps of the education pipeline, particularly for lower-income students.

## Persistence Effects

In addition to encouraging student entry into college, receipt of financial aid enables greater persistence throughout a student's undergraduate career, the next steps along the education pipeline. Financial aid affects persistence decisions positively by maintaining equilibrium between the net price of attending college and the perceived economic returns of attaining a degree. Persistence effects can be measured reductions in dropout rates, transfer rates from community colleges to four-year institutions, and institutional investment in need-based student aid. Positive effects on persistence are particularly important in determining the effectiveness of aid programs because the benefits of higher education cannot be fully realized if students are unable to graduate and obtain degrees.

Jensen (1981) and Murdock (1987) found that financial aid promotes student persistence. As with matriculation findings, financial aid is more effective for lower-income students' persistence than for the persistence of students from other income categories. In a 1995 study, the General Accounting Office found a 14 percent reduction in the dropout probability of lower-income students with the addition of a $1,000 grant (U.S. General Accounting Office, 1995). Moreover, this study found that if grants were targeted to first-year lower-income students, an additional $1,000 in grant aid reduced their probability of dropping out in the first year by 23 percent.

Financial aid also has the positive impact of allowing lower-income students to behave in the same academic and social manner as their non-financially constrained peers. In 1986 Stampen and Cabrera presented a hypothesis, later shown to be valid in Murdock's meta-analysis (1987), that the persistence behavior between lower-income and other students should be the same when adequate financial aid is awarded to the lower-income students. Financial aid equalizes opportunity because it reduces financial reasons for dropping out (Stampen & Cabrera, 1988). In fact, Stampen and Cabrera showed that financial aid effectively compensates for financial disadvantage because it makes lower-income students as likely to persist as their non-financially constrained peers (Stampen & Cabrera, 1988). In addition, having adequate financial resources inspires other positive, non-financial behaviors (e.g., better academic performance, motivation, and relationships with peers) that ultimately lead to greater retention and degree completion in colleges (Stampen & Cabrera, 1987).

Other evidence of the effectiveness of the financial aid programs comes from the greater probability that aid recipients are more likely to transfer from a community college to a four-year campus than are non-recipients (Murdock, 1987). Since attendance at a four-year institution is necessary for the attainment of a bachelor's degree, the impact of financial aid on transfer rates is extremely important.

When considering the effectiveness of financial aid programs, researchers often debate which programs best promote persistence. Specifically, researchers have found that grants are more effective than loans at keeping students, particularly those from lower-income families, in college (U.S. General Accounting Office, 1995; Jensen, 1981; Stampen & Cabrera, 1987). In general, lower-income students are very responsive to grants, whereas loans and work-study programs do not have as large an impact (Terenzini, Cabrera, & Bernal, 2001). The type of aid available also affects the actions of higher education institutions. Without federal financial aid programs, private colleges in particular might reduce their commitments to educating lower-income students (McPherson, 1988). Lacking federal aid for lower-income students, such institutions, which are in intense competition for students, might divert their own aid budgets away from lower-income students and toward middle- and upper-income students with little need for financial aid; that is, in the absence of federal financial aid programs, institutions would be tempted to use their own institutional financial aid money for middle-class choice instead of for lower-income access (McPherson, 1988; McPherson & Schapiro, 1999). Like institutions, states, too, could have similar incentives to end their commitments to open-access institutions without federal aid (McPherson, 1988). Therefore, from the viewpoints of students, institutions, and states, the persistence steps of the education pipeline show not only that they are positively influenced by financial aid but that these steps are also particularly sensitive to the type of financial aid available, favoring grants over loans.

Whether the researchers look at enrollment or persistence effects of financial aid, the general conclusion is clear: Financial aid programs enable lower-income students to complete the educational pipeline and graduate from college. Although federal financial aid programs may be inadequately funded and therefore unable to fully achieve their goal, the programs have provided college access to millions of students and have the potential to further reduce the current inequities in college access.

## TODAY'S ACCESS CHALLENGES

Despite the federal financial aid programs' current and potential future success in addressing unequal educational opportunity, today's college students, particularly lower-income students, continue to face enormous financial barriers to attending, persisting, and graduating from college. In presenting data that measure the current challenges facing students seeking access to higher education, this final section of the chapter considers the enormity of the task facing the federal financial aid programs in promoting access. In addition, this section provides a financial analysis of the programs and also considers the role academic preparation plays in enabling access.

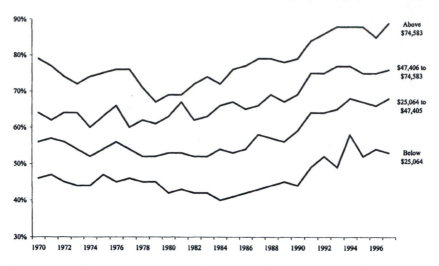

*Figure 1.2  College Participation Rates for Unmarried 18- to 24-Year-Old High School Graduates, by Family Income Quartile, 1970 to 1997*

*Source:* College Board (1999).

## The Current State of Access

One method for measuring access to college today is to consider various factors that correspond to different stages within the education pipeline. Specifically, the enrollment and persistence stages of the pipeline can be gauged by considering college participation rates, and the bachelor's degree completion stage of the pipeline can be considered by analyzing graduation rates. In addition, the adequacy of funding disbursement by financial aid programs can be measured by looking at unmet need. Finally, a discussion of impending demographic forces will foreshadow the challenges policymakers will encounter over the next fifteen years.

A measure of the enrollment and persistence stages of the education pipeline is college participation rates over time. The gap in participation rates between the lowest-income and highest-income families in 1970, for example, stood at 32 percentage points. In 1997, despite an increase in the college-going rate for families in all income ranges, the gap remained at 32 percentage points (Figure 1.2). Unfortunately, over the thirty-year period little progress had been made in reducing this gap and enhancing access for lower-income students.

As striking as these participation gaps are, suggesting significantly less opportunity for lower-income Americans, the gap in achievement of bachelor's degrees was far wider. In 1998, only 6 percent of students with the

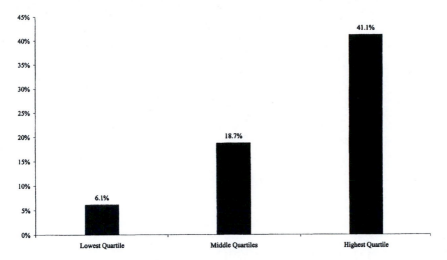

*Figure 1.3 Percentage of 1989 Beginning Postsecondary Students Who Received a Bachelor's Degree or Higher as of 1994, by Family Socioeconomic Status*

Source: Advisory Committee on Student Financial Assistance (2000) and U.S. Department of Education (1996).

lowest socioeconomic status earned a bachelor's degree, compared to 40 percent of those from families with the highest socioeconomic status (Figure 1.3). Since the goals of federal higher education policy are most fully accomplished when students earn a bachelor's degree, a measure of the graduation stage of the education pipeline is a critical marker of the state of access in America.

Unmet need—the amount of money students and families must procure to afford college after all financial aid and expected family contribution are considered—is an important barrier for the nation's poorest students and an indirect measure of the inadequacy of the funding for federal student aid programs. On average, the lowest-income students in 1995 faced $3,200 of unmet need annually at community colleges. At four-year public institutions, they faced average unmet need of $3,800, and at four-year private institutions this amount was over $6,000 (Table 1.1). In comparison, middle- and high-income students faced much lower levels of unmet need at each type of institution.

When thought of as a measure of the adequacy of funding being disbursed by financial aid programs, unmet need shows that it is difficult to fully achieve access for all students. For a lower-income family, nearly $4,000 of unmet need at a four-year public institution is particularly devastating. For most of these families this average amount of unmet need equals one-sixth

Table 1.1
Annual Unmet Need, by Institution Type and Family Income, 1995

| Institution Type | Family Income | | |
|---|---|---|---|
| | Low | Middle | High |
| Public Two–Year | $3,200 | $1,650 | $100 |
| Public Four–Year | $3,800 | $2,250 | $400 |
| Private Four–Year | $6,200 | $4,700 | $3,000 |

Source: U.S. Department of Education (1999).

of their *total* income. From the data, it is quite apparent that excessive unmet need is forcing many lower-income students to choose levels of enrollment and financing alternatives not conducive to academic success, persistence, and, ultimately, degree completion at any institution type.

To make matters worse, the current challenges that higher education and in particular federal financial aid programs face will become more difficult with impending demographic forces (see Chapter 8 for more on demographics). Rivaling the size of the baby boom generation, the projected national growth in the traditional college-age population between 2000 and 2015 will exceed 16 percent, with 1.6 million additional students expected to enroll in college. About 60 percent of this growth is expected to occur among the traditional college-age population. This demographic growth will dramatically increase the overall number of students on America's campuses by nearly 3 million, pushing total enrollment to about 16 million. In its diversity, however, this new generation will reshape higher education, as 80 percent of its members will be non-white. The enormity of these demographics will exacerbate increases in college costs and create a substantial challenge for policymakers.

As measurements of different stages of the education pipeline, participation rates and graduation rates ascertain the enormity of the challenge students face in achieving access. These rates, coupled with the measurable shortfall in resources as measured by unmet need and demographic trends, suggest that in promoting access to higher education, policymakers are currently facing immense challenges that show no signs of abating.

## Role of Academic Preparation

Some policy researchers have claimed that most lower-income students do not attend postsecondary education or persist because they are academically ill-prepared.[10] The logical conclusion of this argument is that federal financial aid programs would have little or no effect in enhancing success in college. Although academic preparation is a necessary condition for entry to college, without adequate finances it can never be a sufficient condition. Even the best-prepared lower-income students—for example, those who score in the top quartile on tests such as the SAT—entered college immediately after graduation from high school at rates nearly 20 percentage points lower than those of their highest-income peers. Indeed, the college-going rate of the highest-socioeconomic-status students with the lowest achievement levels is the same level as the poorest students with the highest achievement levels (Table 1.2). Even these numbers cannot fully capture the current state of access as the most highly qualified lower-income students, based on curricula, test scores, and class rank, attend four-year institutions—a necessary step toward attainment of a bachelor's degree—at a rate that is nearly a third lower than that of their high-income peers.

At every critical stage in the path toward enrollment, data show persistent gaps in the participation of students by income level, even when controlling for academic preparation. Lower-income eighth-grade students are 25 points less likely to expect to finish college in eighth grade (Figure 1.4). As high school seniors, that gap remains unchanged. A 29-point gap exists in students who take entrance exams and apply to college by level of unmet need. By the time final enrollment decisions are made by academically qualified students, those with low unmet need (high income) are 31 points more likely to attend college than are students with high unmet need (lower income)—83 versus 52 percent.

These data suggest that large numbers of low- and moderate-income high school graduates who are academically qualified to attend four-year colleges face high levels of unmet need and either do not enroll in college at all or enroll in lower-cost institutions. Twenty-two percent of college-qualified lower-income high school graduates do not attend college. Thus, high levels of unmet need deny the opportunity of higher education to over 90,000 lower-income college-qualified high school graduates.[11] In addition, approximately 200,000 academically qualified lower-income high

Table 1.2
Percentage of 1992 High School Graduates Attending College in 1994 by
Achievement Test and Socioeconomic Status Quartile

| Achievement Quartile | SES Quartile | |
|---|---|---|
| | Lowest | Highest |
| **Highest** | 78% | 97% |
| **Lowest** | 36% | 77% |

*Source:* Lee (1999).

school graduates fail to attend a four-year college at any point in their academic careers (Advisory Committee on Student Financial Assistance,
2001). In combination with demographic growth, school reform efforts will
likely result in increased levels of academic preparation, significantly en-
larging this pool of academically qualified, but disenfranchised lower-income youth over the next decade.

These analyses demonstrate that academic preparation is a necessary
condition for entry into college, but it is not sufficient. Without adequate
financial resources, academically qualified students are unable to gain access to higher education, especially a four-year institution. The conclusion
is inescapable: No matter how strong the nation's commitment to academic
preparation and no matter how quickly it advances, no progress can be
made toward improved access without a simultaneous commitment to dramatically reducing the financial barrier lower-income students face.

Whether one examines measures of the education pipeline, considers
the funding shortfall of the financial aid programs, or explores issues of academic preparation, the current challenge for achieving equal access is substantial. Considered in conjunction with impending demographic forces,
the future challenge will undoubtedly test policymakers and strain federal
financial aid programs.

## CONCLUSION

The partnership the federal government entered into with states and
higher education institutions to ensure that all Americans could have access to higher education without regard to their economic means has been
a policy success. Measurements at every step along the education pipeline

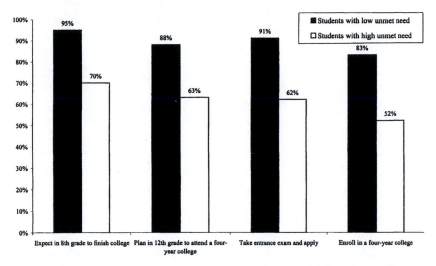

*Figure 1.4 Sequential Impact of Unmet Need on College Qualified High School Graduates*

*Source:* U.S. Department of Education (1997).

have shown that financial aid programs enhance access. College attendance rates for all Americans are higher today than they were thirty years ago, although the attendance gap between high-income and lower-income students persists. More students are academically prepared to enroll in college than ever before. In addition, tens of millions of Americans who would otherwise not have achieved access to college have attended and earned associate's and bachelor's degrees. Indeed, few researchers would suggest that lower-income students could enroll in higher education today without the availability of federal student aid.

Although today we face access challenges that are similar to those that first led to the creation of the financial aid programs in the 1960s, the stakes for individuals and for our nation have increased. The new knowledge-based economy has made higher education more important than ever: Nearly 60 percent of jobs today require at least some college, and both this percentage and the level of education required is likely to increase (Carnevale & Fry, 2000). Thus, eliminating income-related gaps in postsecondary education would add hundreds of billions of dollars to national income annually. Recent estimates suggest that if the 32-percentage-point gap in the college-going rates of the highest- and lowest-income Americans was narrowed significantly, $230 billion to the gross domestic product and $80 billion in tax revenue would be added (see Chapter 8 for more on these estimates). Failure to expand investments in educational opportunity will rob the economy of the most basic resource necessary to sustain economic growth— namely, highly skilled workers. The social toll will be heavy as well, since stratification increases as students who are unable to attend college are consigned to low-paying jobs with declining real wages.

Despite the challenges, recent policy trends indicate a shift in focus away from need-based federal student aid programs. The most predominant policy solution from the 1990s was captured in the creation of tax credits for higher education that have a focus fundamentally different than that of the traditional aid programs.[12] The impact of tax credits was analyzed in a recent report, which indicated that few lower-income students benefited from the program, whereas middle-class students, who would otherwise engage in postsecondary education, received the greatest benefits (Wolanin, 2001). By directing federal assistance away from lower-income students, these programs undermine the federal higher education policy goal of narrowing the unacceptable income-related gaps existing in postsecondary participation, persistence, and degree completion. The concern is that these new programs will come to displace the grants and loans that have been used over the past thirty years in effectively and efficiently delivering aid to lower-income students. Another disturbing policy trend is to focus exclusively on academic preparation—in effect, to blame the lack of student access on academic qualifications rather than financial constraints. As stated earlier, however, both adequate finances and appropriate academic preparation are necessary conditions for access to postsecondary education.

For lower-income students, today's college costs represent a significant barrier to attaining a postsecondary education. Unfortunately, demographics and college costs will continue to place pressure on these students in the future. Over the next fifteen years, policymakers will face serious challenges to the national commitment to providing access to postsecondary education, especially a bachelor's degree. With the increased importance of higher education in today's society, fulfilling federal policy goals for higher education will be a substantial and significant challenge.

Policymakers face two broad challenges today, challenges not unlike the trials their predecessors faced in 1965. First are the competing interests that divert attention from the ideal of equal access to postsecondary education. Second is an ever-increasing demand for need-based financial assistance for college. Given these challenges, the proven system of federal financial aid, which has served the nation so well for the past three decades and has led to measurable increases in access at every stage of the education pipeline, must become an integral part of the future of federal higher education policy. The manner and depth of responses by federal and state policymakers and institutional decisionmakers will determine the level of access to higher education enjoyed by the next generation of Americans.

## NOTES

The views expressed in this chapter are those of the authors, and no official support by the Advisory Committee on Student Financial Assistance or other government entity is intended or should be inferred.

1. For the purposes of this chapter, "lower-income" refers to families whose total annual income is less than $25,000 per year.

2. Although recognizing the importance of state and institutional policymakers, this chapter focuses primarily on the role of the federal government in higher education policy.

3. Although an important current and future issue to many state and institutions, a discussion of institutional capacity building is beyond the scope of this chapter.

4. For a more detailed discussion of positive externalities and policy justifications for federal financial aid, see Wolanin (2001).

5. Although it is important to the development of federal higher education policy, a discussion of the federal government's role in the support of institutional research is beyond the scope of this chapter.

6. Although the Guaranteed Student Loan (GSL) program created by the 1965 act is the only true student aid entitlement, the Pell Grant is often called an entitlement because it operates in a manner similar to other federal entitlements; that is, all recipients who are equally qualified receive the same level of grant. However, in contrast to true federal entitlements such as Medicare, the maximum Pell Grant is set annually through appropriations from domestic discretionary expenditures and has historically been less than the authorized limit.

7. For a comprehensive review of the issues presented here, see Terenzini, Cabrera, and Bernal (2001).

8. A starting point to look at this area of research is to focus on the fields of sociology of education and student development theory.

9. For a more detailed explanation of the various models that researchers used to predict enrollment effects based on financial aid and tuition, see Jackson and Weathersby (1975) and Heller (1997).

10. See, for example, National Commission on the High School Senior Year (2001).

11. Lee (2001) estimates that between 80,000 and 140,000 academically qualified low-SES students (using slightly different definitions of preparation) did not attend college and nearly 200,000 such students did not attend four-year institutions.

12. For a comprehensive review of the tax programs, see Spencer (1999) and Wolanin (2001).

## REFERENCES

Advisory Committee on Student Financial Assistance (2000). *Access denied: Restoring the nation's commitment to equal educational opportunity.* Washington, DC: Author.

Advisory Committee on Student Financial Assistance (2001). *Estimating the impact of unmet need on college qualified students.* Washington, DC: Author.

Carnevale, A. P., & Fry, R. A. (2000). *Crossing the great divide: Can we achieve equity when Generation Y goes to college?* ETS Leadership 2000 Series. Princeton, NJ: Educational Testing Service.

Choy, S. P., & Ottinger, C. (November 1998). *Choosing a postsecondary institution.* Statistical Analysis Report, NCES 98–080. Washington, DC: U.S. Department of Education, Office of Educational Research and Improvement, National Center for Education Statistics.

College Board. (1999). *Trends in college pricing, 1999.* Washington, DC: Author.

College Board. (2001a). *Trends in college pricing, 2001.* Washington, DC: Author.

College Board. (2001b). *Trends in student aid, 2001.* Washington, DC: Author.

*Congressional Record,* daily. August 26, 1965, pp. H21092–93.

Ellis, J. (2001). *Founding brothers: The revolutionary generation.* New York: Alfred A. Knopf.

Flint, T. A. (1992). Parental and planning influences on the formation of student college choice sets. *Research in Higher Education,* 33(6), 689–708.

Gladieux, L. E., & Wolanin, T. R. (1976). *Congress and the colleges: The national politics of higher education.* Lexington, MA: Lexington Books.

Heller, D. E. (1997). Student price response in higher education: An update to Leslie and Brinkman. *Journal of Higher Education,* 33(6), 657–87.

Hofstadter, R. & Smith, W. (eds.). (1961). *American higher education: A documentary history.* Vol. 1. Chicago: University of Chicago Press.

Hossler, D., Schmit, J., & Vesper, N. (1999). *Going to college: How social, economic, and educational factors influence the decisions students make.* Baltimore, MD: Johns Hopkins University Press.

Jackson, G. A. (1978). Financial aid and student enrollment. *Journal of Higher Education,* 49(6), 549–74.

Jackson, G. A., & Weathersby, G. B. (1975). Individual demand for higher education: A review and analysis of recent empirical studies. *Journal of Higher Education,* 46(6), 623–52.

Jensen, E. L. (1981). Student financial aid and persistence in college. *Journal of Higher Education,* 52(3), 280–94.

Johnstone, D. B. (1995, October). Starting points: Fundamental assumptions underlying the principles and policies of federal financial aid to students. Conference on the Best Ways for the Federal Government to Help Students and Families Financial Postsecondary Education. Charleston, SC: U.S. Department of Education.

King, J. E. (1996). *The decision to go to college: Attitudes and experiences associated with college attendance among low-income students*. Washington, DC: College Board.

Lee, J. B. (1999). How do students and families pay for college? In J. E. King (ed.), *Financing a college education: How it works, how it's changing*. Phoenix, AZ: American Council on Education and Oryx Press.

Lee, J. B. (2001, October). Access for low SES students. Presentation at National Governors Association Center for Best Practices, Washington, DC.

Leslie, L. L., Johnson, G. P., & Carlson, J. (1977). The impact of need-based student aid upon the college attendance decision. *Journal of Education Finance*, 2, 269–85.

Mann, H. (1867). *Lectures and annual reports*. Edited by Mary Mann. Cambridge, MA: Author.

Manski, C. F., & Wise, D. A. (1983). *College choice in America*. Cambridge, MA: Harvard University Press.

McPherson, M. S. (1988). On assessing the impact of federal student aid. *Economics of Education Review*, 7(1), 77–84.

McPherson, M. S., & Schapiro, M. O. (1998). *The student aid game: Meeting need and rewarding talent in American higher education*. Princeton, NJ: Princeton University Press.

McPherson, M. S., & Schapiro, M. O. (1999, May). Reinforcing stratification in American higher education: Some disturbing trends. Macalester Forum on Higher Education Conference, Diversity and Stratification in American Higher Education, St. Paul, MN.

Miller, E. I. (1997). Parents' views on the value of a college education and how they will pay for it. *Journal of Student Financial Aid*, 27(1), 20.

Murdock, T. A. (1987). It isn't just money: The effects of financial aid on student persistence. *Review of Higher Education*, 11(1), 75–101.

National Commission on the High School Senior Year (2001). *Raising our sights: No high school senior left behind*. Princeton, NJ: Woodrow Wilson National Fellowship Foundation.

Olson, L., & Rosenfeld, R. A. (1984). Parents and the process of gaining access to student financial aid. Journal of Higher Education, 55(4), 455–80.

President's Commission on Higher Education. (1947). *Higher education for American democracy*. New York: Harper & Bros.

Rainsford, G. N. (1972). *Congress and higher education in the nineteenth century*. Knoxville: University of Tennessee Press.

Rivlin, A. M. (1961). *The role of the federal government in financing higher education*. Washington, DC: Brookings Institution.

Rivlin, A. M. (1970). Equality of opportunity. In *financing equal opportunity in higher education*. New York: College Entrance Examination Board.

St. John, E. P. (1994a). Assessing tuition and student aid strategies: Using price-response measures to simulate pricing alternatives. *Research in Higher Education*, 35(3), 301–35.

St. John, E. P. (1994b). *Prices, productivity, and investment: Assessing financial strategies in higher education*. ASHE-ERIC Higher Education Reports, No. 3. Washington, DC: George Washington University, ERIC Clearinghouse on Higher Education.

St. John, E. P., Paulsen, M. B., & Starkey, J. B. (1996). The nexus between college choice and persistence. *Research in Higher Education*, 30(6), 563–81.

Spencer, A. C. (1999). New politics of higher education. In J. E. King (ed.), *Financing a college education: How it works, how it's changing*. Phoenix, AZ: American Council on Education and Oryx Press.

Stampen, J. O., & Cabrera, A. F. (1988). The targeting and packaging of student aid and its effect on attrition. *Economics of Education Review*, 7(1), 29–46.

Sundquist, J. L. (1968). *Politics and policy: The Eisenhower, Kennedy, and Johnson years*. Washington, DC: Brookings Institution.

Terenzini, P. T., Cabrera, A. F., & Bernal, E. M. (2001). *Swimming against the tide: The poor in American higher education*. The College Board Research Report No. 2001–1. New York: College Board.

Tierney, M. S. (1980). The impact of financial aid on student demand for public/private higher education. *Journal of Higher Education*, 51(5), 527–45.

U.S. Department of Education (1996). *Descriptive summary of 1989–90 beginning postsecondary students: Five years later*. NCES 96–155. Washington, DC: National Center for Educational Statistics.

U.S. Department of Education (1997). *Access to postsecondary education for the 1992 high school graduates*. NCES 98–105. Washington, DC: National Center for Education Statistics.

U.S. Department of Education. (1999). *College access and affordability: Findings from the condition of education, 1998*. NCES 99–108. Washington, DC: National Center for Educational Statistics.

U.S. General Accounting Office. (1995, March). *Higher education: Restructuring student aid could reduce low-income student dropout rate*. GAO/HEHS-95-48. Washington, DC: Author.

Wolanin, T. R. (2001). *Rhetoric and reality: Effects and consequences of the HOPE scholarship*. New Millennium Project on Higher Education Costs, Pricing, and Productivity. Washington, DC: Institute for Higher Education Policy, Ford Foundation, Education Resources Institute.

# CHAPTER 2

## An Issue of Equity

### John B. Lee

Federal student aid was originally designed to allow students from lower-income families to continue their education at the postsecondary level, thereby ensuring that a lower-income family did not need to make unusual sacrifices to send their child to a public college. Fulfilling this goal translated into federal programs providing grants large enough to pay the reasonable costs of education that would otherwise be beyond the capacity of a lower-income family.

Over the years, the consensus supporting this program purpose has dissipated. Affordability for middle-income families has displaced the original goal of providing access to students who would otherwise not be able to attend college at all, as the burgeoning federal loan programs and tuition tax credits benefiting students across a broad income range attests. In addition, some states have elected to put less emphasis on financial need as a criterion for awarding grants, channeling money to middle- and upper-income families.

This analysis measures the adequacy of student aid as it currently operates to provide access and choice to students with differing financial resources. It also provides a framework for describing a federal grant program designed to restore the original national goal of equal access to higher education.

## ACCESS AND CHOICE

A working definition of access means that a lower-income student should be financially able to attend a four-year public college and live on campus.

This benchmark goes beyond providing access to the lowest-cost education possible, but it stops short of suggesting that the federal government should provide the resources necessary to allow any student to attend any post-secondary institution.

## Characteristics of Lower-Income Students

Most studies confirm that lower-income dependent college-age youth are less likely to attend college and, if they do attend, are less likely to graduate than are higher-income undergraduates (U.S. Department of Education, 2000). Low income is often associated with other factors that influence enrollment of college-age youth, such as parents who have not gone to college and inadequate high school preparation. It is difficult to disentangle these background factors from income.

Despite these corollary characteristics, Donald E. Heller has demonstrated that lower-income dependent undergraduates are more sensitive to changes in the price of attendance than are higher-income students, even when relevant background variables are taken into consideration (Heller, 1999, and Chapter 4 of this volume). Increasing the net price of attendance reduces the probability that lower-income students will enroll in college. Similarly, St. John has shown that student aid makes a difference in the persistence of lower-income dependent undergraduates (St. John, 2000). The higher the price of attendance, the less likely lower-income students are to continue their education. While net increases in costs are one factor in the equation, changes in the type, amount, or value of available student aid will also reduce the enrollment of lower income students.

## The Role of Student Aid

Some students from all income backgrounds rely on various types of student aid; however, the role that aid plays is different for low-, middle-, and higher-income students. Over time, loans have become a much larger share of the student aid package (see Chapter 3). Middle- or upper-income students may take a loan for convenience or so that they can attend a more expensive institution than would be possible with grants and family support alone. These students are also eligible for, and often receive, merit grants.

However, lower-income students have been increasingly forced to use loans to gain access to college. By definition, this trend reduces the future income of these students by the amount necessary to repay the loan, thus diminishing the value of a college education for a group already concerned about deferring earnings to attend college. In part, this trend is attributable to the decline in the value of grant aid relative to the costs of higher education. Federal grant aid has been expanded to include more recipients, whereas the value of grants available to the lowest-income undergraduates has eroded relative to the price of enrollment (see Chapters 1 and 3).

## METHODS AND DEFINITIONS

This analysis uses data on families that have been classified as low, middle, or high income based on their expected family contribution (EFC) as determined by postsecondary institutions. The EFC is designed to determine how much discretionary income a family can theoretically be expected to contribute toward educational expenses. The formula for calculating EFC is often modified to meet policy needs and provide comparability among very dissimilar families, and thus it represents a set of political and value assumptions. Still, since it takes into account family savings, size, and special expenses, as well as student earnings and savings, the EFC provides a more sensitive measure of a family's wealth and ability to pay for postsecondary education than does family income alone.

The EFC does not, however, consider the actual expenses a family may have at the time a child is ready to start college. A family that is expected to contribute $7,500 annually toward college education may, and often does, find itself with minimal savings or discretionary income because of house payments, car expenses, and other obligations. This common profile makes it impossible for such families to provide the estimated amount for college expenses without sharply reducing living standards. The squeeze translates into powerful political pressure to improve affordability for students from middle-income families. Higher-income families, in contrast, are more likely than others to have savings and discretionary income to support their college-age children.

The analysis is based on dependent undergraduates because the income of independent undergraduates does not necessarily reflect the social and cultural attributes typically associated with lower income. An independent student becomes poor by giving up his or her job to attend college. Thus, the average net cost of college for dependent undergraduates increases as income increases, but among independent undergraduates income and the net cost of attending college are not related. Combining the two groups would mask or distort relationships commonly associated with income.

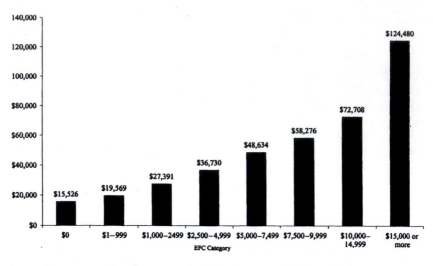

*Figure 2.1 Average Family Income, by EFC Category, 1995–1996*

*Source:* U.S. Department of Education (1996b).

The cost of attendance represents the actual expenses assigned to the student based on the time he or she attended college, including tuition, living expenses (room and board), books, equipment, and other incidental costs. Living expenses vary depending on whether the student lives on campus, at home, or off campus. Part-time students are assigned a pro-rata reduced amount for tuition, living, and other costs. The difference between the price of attendance and the combination of EFC and student aid is defined as "unmet need."

## EXPECTED FAMILY CONTRIBUTION

### EFC and Income

Figure 2.1 shows the relationship between income and expected family contribution.[1] The data source is the 1996 National Postsecondary Student Aid Study (U.S. Department of Education, 1996b), a survey conducted for the National Center for Education Statistics that represents a national sample of undergraduates enrolled in accredited postsecondary institutions in the 1995–1996 academic year. The income estimates provide a general guide, but they are not exact in that families with the same EFC could have different incomes. By our definition, lower-income families can be expected to contribute $1,000 or less toward their child's col-

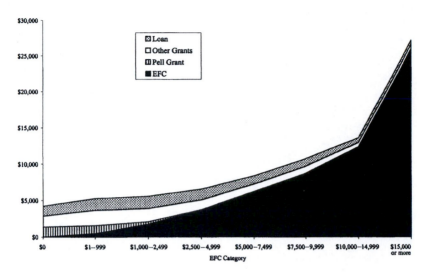

*Figure 2.2 Average Amount of Aid Awarded, by EFC Category, 1995–1996*

Source: U.S. Department of Education (1996b).

lege education, which generally translates into an average income of below $20,000. Middle-income students include those families that could contribute more than $1,000, but less than $10,000. At the top end of the middle-income range, most families would theoretically have the resources to pay for a public four-year college or university without much help from government sources. Families with $10,000 or more projected to contribute toward education costs are defined as high income, beginning at about $72,700 per year.

## Student Aid by EFC

Figure 2.2 shows the average financial aid received by undergraduates in each of the EFC categories (including those within each category that received no aid). The table suggests several conclusions in addition to the obvious point that even after all aid is awarded, lower-income students have less money for college than do higher-income students.

First, lower-income students were more likely to receive Pell Grants than were higher-income students, but grants from states, private agencies, or institutions provided them with more support than did Pell Grants. Second, other grants provided aid to a much broader range of students in terms of family income than did Pell Grants. Third, lower-income students do not bor-

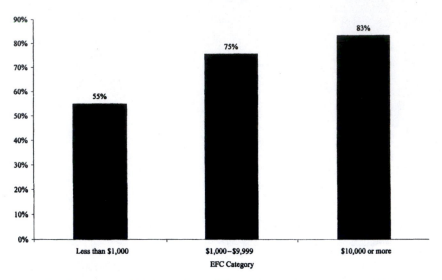

*Figure 2.3 Percentage of Undergraduates Whose Parents Are Married, by EFC Category, 1995–1996*

Source: U.S. Department of Education (1996a).

row more on average than middle-income students, but they do borrow more than higher-income students. Lower- and middle-income students have average annual loans in the range of $1,400 to $1,600, compared with $600 for higher-income students. Fourth, the expected family contribution accelerates for higher-income students, which starts at around $73,000 family income. This reflects the discretionary income available to families in this range.

## LOWER INCOME AND COLLEGE ATTENDANCE

### Characteristics of Lower-Income Families

Lower-income families as defined by this report are more likely than middle- and higher-income families to be headed by a single parent, include a larger than average number of children, and have limited financial resources beyond income. As shown in Figure 2.3, 45 percent of the lower-income students surveyed came from single-parent homes, compared to 17 percent from the highest income group. Single-parent families depend on one adult earner, which suggests a less reliable financial base than a two-parent family.

Similarly, Figure 2.4 shows that lower-income two-parent families were more than twice as likely to have four or more children than were families

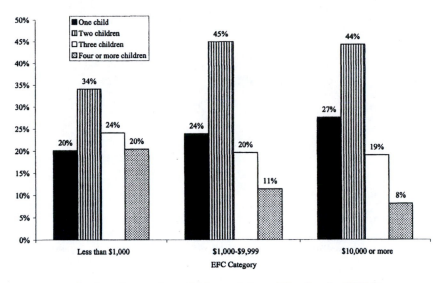

*Figure 2.4 Number of Dependent Children in Married Families, by EFC Category, 1995–1996*

Source: U.S. Department of Education (1996a).

in the highest income range, and were less likely to have only one child than either middle- or higher-income families. Larger families face more unexpected expenses and have less flexibility in dealing with financial crises than do families with fewer children.

It is not surprising that lower-income families have fewer assets in terms of home ownership, savings, and investments than higher-income families, but Figure 2.5 demonstrates the magnitude of the difference. Lower-income families were about one-third less likely to own a home than were higher-income families. The biggest difference in assets is found in the lack of savings or investments of low- and middle-income families compared with higher-income families. However, our data show that relatively few U.S. families with college-age children, in whatever income strata, have $10,000 in liquid assets available to them.

## Enrollment Patterns

The extra effort it takes for a low- or middle-income student to attend college is evident in Figure 2.6, which shows the type of institution in which first-year dependent undergraduates from each of the three income groups enrolled in 1995. Compared with higher-income students, lower-

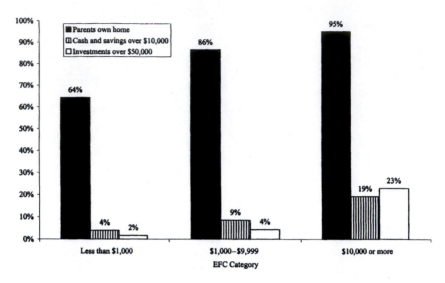

Figure 2.5 Percentage of Families with Assets, by EFC Category, 1995–1996

Source: U.S. Department of Education (1996a).

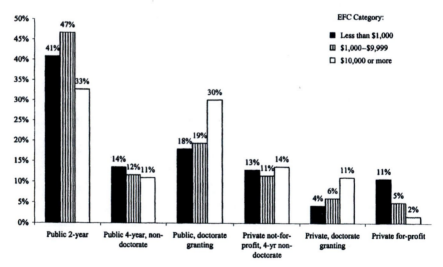

Figure 2.6 Distribution of Beginning Undergraduates, by EFC Category and Institution Type, 1995–1996

Source: U.S. Department of Education (1996a).

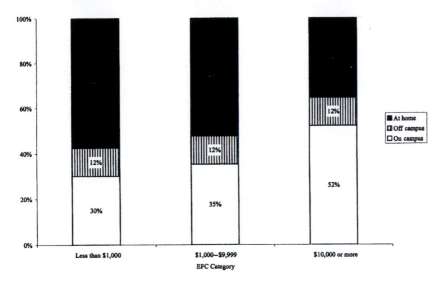

*Figure 2.7 Residence during the First Year of Enrollment, by EFC Category, 1995–1996*

Source: U.S. Department of Education (1996a).

income undergraduates were more likely to start education in a proprietary school or a community college, and less likely to start in either a public or private university. The enrollment profile of lower-income undergraduates is closer to middle-income students than that of middle-income students is to the profile of higher-income students.

## Living Arrangements

One of the compromises lower-income students make to reduce the cost of attendance is living at home. Although students living at home are credited with room-and-board costs in the need-analysis system, the actual out-of-pocket cost is limited compared with living on campus. Even so, living at home reduces the chances of a student persisting because it works against integrating a student with the life of the campus, a factor associated with graduation (Pascarella & Terenzini, 1991). Also, a student who lives at home and works more than twenty hours a week runs a greater risk of dropping out than does the student who lives on campus and works twenty hours or less a week. Figure 2.7 shows that 58 percent of lower-income students studied lived at home, compared with 36 percent of the higher-income students. Conversely, 30 percent of the entering lower-income stu-

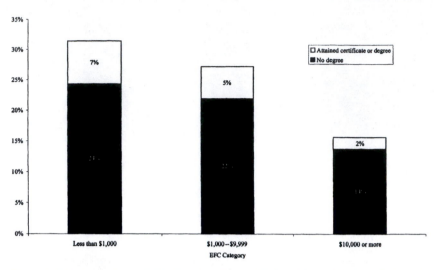

*Figure 2.8 Undergraduates Who First Enrolled in 1995 and Were Not Enrolled as of 1998, by EFC Category*

*Source*: U.S. Department of Education (1996a).

dents lived on campus, compared with 52 percent of the higher-income students.

## Persistence

Figure 2.8 shows the enrollment outcomes in 1998 for those who first enrolled in 1995. Twenty-four percent of the lower-income students had left school without receiving a degree or certificate, compared with 14 percent of the higher-income students. Another 7 percent of the lower-income students were not enrolled in 1998, but they had received a degree or certificate, compared with 2 percent of the higher-income students.[2] These results show that over the first three years of college, nearly twice as many lower-income students had left college without a degree as had higher-income students; higher-income students were much more likely to persist in obtaining a degree.

## Degree Aspiration

Degree aspiration of first-year students increases with income. Figure 2.9 shows that 61 percent of the lower-income students entered college with the

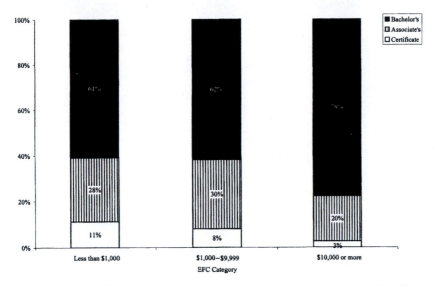

*Figure 2.9 Degree Expectation of Undergraduates at the Time They Entered College, by EFC Category, 1995–1996*

Source: U.S. Department of Education (1996a).

objective of receiving a bachelor's degree, compared with 78 percent of those from the highest income group. This probably reflects the importance of foregone income to lower-income students, as well as social and cultural factors that encourage higher-income students to attain a bachelor's degree. Students from families at the economic margin tend to value early entry into the labor market more highly than do students from more affluent families.

## Reasons for Attending

Figure 2.10 indicates the importance of economic factors in determining college attendance for lower-income students. Nearly twice as many lower-income students said they were going to school because they needed the education to enter the workforce than for the personal satisfaction of earning a degree. Middle- and higher-income students were nearly evenly split between these two reasons. Economic motives thus play an important role in lower-income students' decisions to pursue postsecondary education.

These outcomes lend credibility to the premise that lower-income students are forced to consider their economic needs in setting and pursuing their educational goals. They are less able to afford the luxury of following their intellectual interests than are higher-income students. In some cases

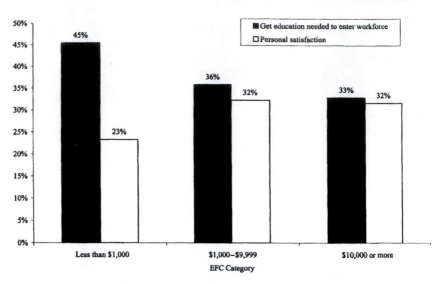

*Figure 2.10 Reasons for Attending College, by EFC Category, 1995–1996*

Source: U.S. Department of Education (1996a).

they are forced to make compromises to save money, such as living at home while they go to college, thus undermining their long-term chances for success.


## MEASURING EQUITY

This study provides the framework for calculating how much grant aid would be needed to equalize resources among students. The model is based on undergraduates attending institutions in a single cost category to control for any variation in cost across the EFC groups that could influence aid awarded and the resulting unmet need. Figure 2.11 shows the actual distribution of aid by EFC category for students attending an institution with a cost of between $10,700 and $11,700 per year (in 1995–1996 dollars), representing access to almost any public college or university in the nation and some independent institutions. The budget provides enough money to live on campus while attending school.

Calculations include all undergraduates, even if they did not receive aid. The data show that lower-income undergraduates who attend institutions in this price range do not have enough money—after combining grants, loans, and what they and their families can be expected to contribute—to pay the full cost. In fact, it is not until the top end of the middle-income

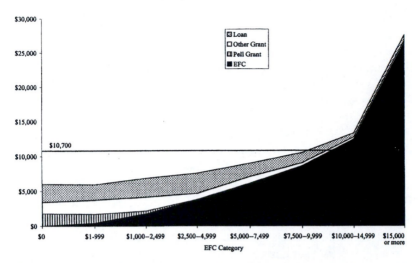

*Figure 2.11 Average Aid Amount for Undergraduates Attending Institutions with a Price of Attendance between $10,700 and $11,700, 1995–1996*

Source: U.S. Department of Education (1996a).

group that the combined aid and expected family contribution provide the full resources necessary to attend. The average undergraduate with a zero family contribution received an aid package consisting of $1,784 in Pell Grants, $1,636 in other grants, and $2,599 in loans, for a total of $6,019. The shortfall, or unmet need, can be calculated by tracing a line across the chart at the cost of attendance. The difference below that line, but above the average amount available to the student through student aid and EFC, represents unmet need.

The first test of equity is that grant aid should be adequate to make up the difference between the price of attendance and EFC. As EFC increases, the grant amount should decline. The second test of equity is that lower-income students should not be forced to borrow more than higher-income students to pay for college. The current financial aid system is inadequate on both counts.

The difference between the price of attendance and the money the poorest undergraduates had available was at least $4,700. The next category of lower-income dependent undergraduates had $6,503, including the expected family contribution, to attend institutions that cost around $11,000. By comparison, the average middle-income student had an EFC of $8,600, and received $424 in grants and $1,461 in loans. Adding EFC to the aid provides them with combined total resources of roughly $10,500, close to the cost of attendance. Not only did middle-income students have more money to pay for education, but they borrowed $1,000 less than lower-income students to attend the same-price institution.

Lower-income undergraduates were forced to borrow more than higher-income students to go to college at this price. Even after loan aid, the magnitude of difference in the financial effort required is so large that doubling the average federal grant for lower-income students would still put them well below what is required to reach equity. Figure 2.11 shows that even with all aid included, lower-income dependent undergraduates did not have the resources to fully cover their college costs. Their attendance at all under these conditions indicates the importance lower-income students place on education as a vehicle to future well-being.

Selecting a lower cost point to define access does not change the picture for lower-income dependent undergraduates. Figure 2.12 shows the resources available for undergraduates paying between $4,750 and $5,750, which would allow a student to live at home and attend a low-tuition public college. Financial aid does not even pay half the cost of attending the lowest-priced colleges in America for lower-income undergraduates.

The lowest-income undergraduates received $2,130 in aid to attend colleges with a cost of attendance of around $5,250. On average, these undergraduates received $1,456 in Pell Grants, $400 in other grants, and $265 in loans. The lowest-income students with no family contribution attending lower-priced institutions were short approximately $3,100 after they received all their aid. Undergraduates in the $1,000 EFC category received $1,969 in aid to pay for college, which was not significantly different than those with no EFC.

The biggest difference in aid for these undergraduates and those attending higher-cost institutions is the limited use of loans. Even though middle-income undergraduates with an EFC of $6,200 should be able to attend a college in this price range with no trouble, they received an average of $295 in grants and $220 in loans. In both of these cases, the gap between available resources and price of attendance defines the extra grant aid that would fully support the student.

The gap narrows as expected family contribution increases. The difference between the price of attendance and the sum of all aid plus expected family contribution represents unmet need, which translates into extra family effort. Family effort (beyond the EFC) signifies some mix of actions that allows a student to attend college when he or she does not have the needed financial support. Examples might include a real reduction in family standard of living, extra work by the student, living at home to reduce living costs, or a lower standard of living for the student. Middle-income undergraduates and wealthier undergraduates do not need to make this effort to attend college.

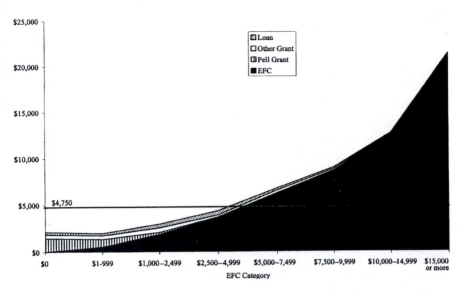

Figure 2.12 *Average Aid Amount for Undergraduates Attending Institutions with a Price of Attendance between $4,750 and $5,750, 1995–1996*

Source: U.S. Department of Education (1996a).

## CONCLUSIONS

Expected family contribution provides the cornerstone of this analysis. The EFC offers guidance to financial aid professionals on how to distribute aid, but it seems to lack political relevance. Political decisions are energized by expressions of felt need, which is defined as the gap between college expenses and the surplus money left over beyond basic needs. Felt need, or affordability for middle-income families, has become increasingly important in the political calculation, whereas addressing the current unmet need of lower-income students defined by EFC has ebbed in importance.

Financial concerns influence lower-income students' every experience with college. More lower-income students enroll in college with hopes of improving their financial condition than do higher-income students. Lower-income students are more likely to aspire to a degree below the baccalaureate, presumably so they can enter the labor market sooner.

Such students are also more likely than higher-income students to leave college without attaining any degree, for lack of financial resources and compromises such as living at home tend to decrease the likelihood of their staying in college. Presumably, adequate funding of grant programs would increase the chances that these students would persist in their college careers by freeing them from some of the financial pressures and related choices they are forced to make to afford college.

As suggested in Figure 2.11, using the EFC to achieve equity of access for students attending an institution priced between $10,700 and $11,700 would require larger grant awards for lower-income students, but it would also spread grants up the income scale to students with a family income approaching $58,000. Increasing the maximum grants to approximately $10,000 and increasing the number of students who receive a grant would achieve equity, and the policy would also improve affordability for lower-middle-income students.

Two issues need to be addressed if this model of equity is to be used as a guide. The first is the possibility that increased grant aid would provide an incentive to raise tuition at public institutions. The second is the political problem posed by providing large grants to lower-income families while expecting middle-income families to provide the majority of their own support.

The first of these concerns could be addressed if states were engaged as partners with the Department of Education in improving access. If federal grants provided access to lower-income students attending public institutions up to the average public tuition level, states with higher-than-average public tuition could provide their own grants to fill this gap. Such an agreement would provide access for lower-income students while minimizing the incentives for states to raise tuition in public colleges and universities. The more broadly available subsidies provided through loans and tax credits provide greater incentives for states and colleges to raise tuition than does aid that is limited to lower-income students.

The second concern can be minimized by expanding the maximum grant awards to middle-income students. Targeting the middle class will increase the political support for student grants.

The most important contribution of the approach outlined in this chapter is a template that provides clear guidance for state and federal policymakers concerned with the allocation of student financial aid. The approach also provides a way to link state and federal financial aid policy, two realms discussed further in Chapters 3 and 4.

## NOTES

1. The EFC categories selected provide enough cases to minimize sampling error in the results.

2. Because the timeframe (three years) was too short for most students to earn a bachelor's degree, these students were recipients of associate's degrees or sub-baccalaureate certificates.

# REFERENCES

Educational Resources Institute. (1998, November). *Do grants matter? Student grant aid and college affordability.* Boston, MA: Author.

Heller, D. E. (1999). The effects of tuition and state financial aid on public college enrollment. *Review of Higher Education, 23*(1), 65–89.

Pascarella, E. T., & Terenzini, P. T. (1991). *How college affects students.* San Francisco: Jossey-Bass Publishers.

St. John, E. P. (2000, October). Financial aid packaging and debt burden: High tuition/high loans and educational opportunity. Presentation at the Student Loan Repayment Symposium. Washington, DC: U.S. Department of Education, Office of Student Financial Assistance.

U.S. Department of Education, National Center for Education Statistics. (1994, September). *Undergraduates who work while enrolled in postsecondary education: 1989–90.* Washington, DC: Author.

U.S. Department of Education, National Center for Education Statistics. (1996a). *Beginning postsecondary students survey, 1995–98.* Washington, DC: Author.

U.S. Department of Education, National Center for Education Statistics. (1996b). *National postsecondary student aid study survey, 1995–96.* Washington, DC: Author.

U.S. Department of Education, National Center for Education Statistics. (1998, November). *Student financing of undergraduate education: 1995–96.* Washington, DC: Author.

U.S. Department of Education, National Center for Education Statistics. (2000, March). *Low-income students: Who they are and how they pay for their education.* Washington, DC: Author.

# PART II

## Student Aid Programs

# CHAPTER 3

# Federal Student Aid in Historical Perspective

*Lawrence E. Gladieux*

More than fifty years ago, the GI Bill demonstrated to skeptics in both government and academia that higher education could and should serve a much wider segment of society than had previously been the case. In 1965, Congress passed the Higher Education Act and committed the federal government to the goal of opening college doors to all, regardless of family income or wealth. Historically, the federal government has led the nation in trying to broaden access to higher education. Today federal programs generate nearly three-fourths of all aid available to help students and families pay for postsecondary education.

Access to postsecondary education, however, remains sharply unequal in America. This chapter examines the continuing discrepancies in postsecondary opportunity, trends in college pricing, and perceptions and politics surrounding the affordability of higher education. I argue that changes in federal policy over the past two decades have shifted attention, incentives, and revenues away from students least able to afford postsecondary education—students for whom financial assistance is most likely to make a difference in their decision and ability to enroll in college. Targeted, need-based aid is the federal government's most effective strategy to expand individual opportunity and boost the country's net investment in higher education.

## PROGRESS, BUT PERSISTENT GAPS

For most of the last half-century, access to some form of postsecondary education has grown steadily—overall, and for nearly every economic and racial or ethnic group. Sheer economic incentives have driven this growth; forces running deep in our economy have ratcheted up skill and credential requirements in the job market, placing a premium on education beyond high school.

Although there are no guarantees in life with or without a college diploma, the odds are increasingly stacked against those with the least education and training. On average, earnings correlate positively with years of formal education. More important, U.S. census data show that the earnings advantage of the most highly educated workers increased during the 1980s and 1990s (U.S. Bureau of the Census, 2000). These trends have become conventional wisdom. People understand that college—and often which college and which course of study—determines the best jobs and life chances.

The good news is that more people are attaining higher levels of education and filling millions of skilled, high-paying jobs generated by a booming economy. The bad news is that opportunities for education remain unequal across society. Wage and wealth disparities have reached extremes unprecedented in our nation's recent history, and the least educated and skilled are getting a smaller and smaller piece of the pie. Education and training alone will not solve structural problems in the employment system that are tending to widen gaps between rich and poor. Yet it is clear that postsecondary education is more important than ever, to the individual and to our society.

Federal aid, along with state and private student aid, has helped fuel a half-century of explosive growth in college attendance and educational attainment. Colleges and universities in the United States now enroll 15 million students, 1.5 times the number registered in 1965, six times the enrollment in 1950, and ten times pre–World War II levels (U.S. Department of Education, 2001). The proportion of the population 25 to 29 years of age that has completed four years of college or more has quadrupled since 1940. Yet large disparities persist in access to higher education in America.

## Who Goes to College, and Where Do They Attend?

Public policy has done a good job of boosting entry into the system. All groups show gains. As shown in Chapter 1, however, lower- and moderate-income students attend college at much lower rates than do middle- and upper-income students, and participation gaps today are as wide, if not wider, than they were twenty-five years ago.

Institutional choice is also closely linked to a student's family background. The most recent longitudinal data from the U.S. Department of Education show that only one of five students from the lowest socioeconomic quartile who attends college enrolls in a four-year institution, compared to two of three from the highest quartile (U.S. Department of Education, 1997a). The data suggest that the most disadvantaged students are increasingly concentrated at community colleges.

This is not to say that the bachelor's degree is the only measure of parity—far from it. "Going to college" means many things and produces many outcomes. We need a range of sub-baccalaureate opportunities, providing skills and credentials for survival and success in a complex economy. But the reality is that students attending less than four-year schools reap lower economic rewards on average than those who end up with a bachelor's degree or more.

## Who Completes?

The most important question is whether students complete their programs, at whatever level, and receive their degree or certificate. Some students fall short of a degree, yet go on to productive careers. However, our economy and labor markets rely heavily on credentials and the skills they signal to employers.

Although postsecondary participation has soared during the past quarter-century, the proportion of college students completing degrees of any kind has remained flat. Given the growing diversity of students and the increasing complexity of their attendance patterns (more part-time, intermittent, and multiple-institution enrollments), stable completion rates may be more than we could have reasonably expected. However, we need to do much better.

According to data from the U.S. Department of Education, roughly three-quarters of high school seniors go on to some form of postsecondary education (U.S. Department of Education, 2001). Half receive some type of degree within five years of entering postsecondary education, and about one-quarter receive a bachelor's degree or higher. However, the most socioeconomically advantaged students graduate at much higher rates than their less advantaged counterparts. Also, white students are considerably more likely to receive a bachelor's degree than are black and Hispanic students.

Getting students in the door is not good enough. Along with young people who do not finish high school and those who stop their education with

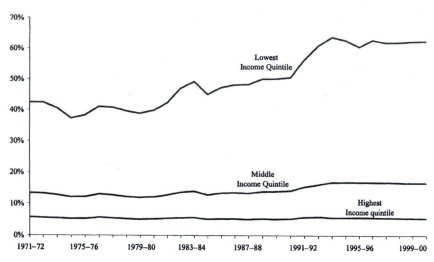

*Figure 3.1 Average Cost of Attendance of Four-Year Public Institutions as a Share of Family Income, 1972–1973 to 1999–2000*

Source: College Board (2000).

a high school diploma, many postsecondary noncompleters fall into what has been called "the forgotten half" of America's youth and young adult population (Halperin, 1998). In fact, some of these students may be left worse off if they have borrowed to finance their studies—increasingly the case for lower-income students—and do not complete their programs. They leave college with no degree, few skills, and student loan debt to repay.

## ECONOMIC AND POLICY TRENDS

Why do discrepancies in postsecondary opportunity remain so wide? The media, policymakers, and the general public have focused attention on the decline in the affordability of higher education, with good reason. Alarm is rooted in economic trends since 1980. Changes in tuition prices, family incomes, and financial aid policy have fallen hardest on those with the least ability to pay.

Tuition—the sticker price of higher education—remained nearly flat in the 1970s when adjusted for inflation, then soared after 1980. According to the College Board, average, inflation-adjusted tuition prices have more than doubled for both public and private four-year institutions since 1980. During this same period, median family income was nearly stagnant, ris-

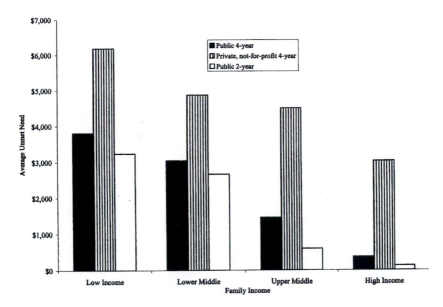

*Figure 3.2 Unmet Need, by Institutional Type and Family Income Group, 1995–1996*

*Source:* U.S. Department of Education (1998).

ing less than 25 percent. Student aid increased in total value, but not enough to keep up with the rise in tuition (College Board, 2000).

Median family income, moreover, tells only part of the story because incomes have grown steadily less equal during the past two decades. Figure 3.1 shows that the costs of college attendance as a share of income have increased for many families, but they have gone up the most for those in the lower-income ranges. For a lower-income family, the average price of attending a public four-year institution represented 62 percent of income in 1999, up from 42 percent in 1971.[1] For a middle-income family, such costs represented 17 percent of income in 1999, compared to 12 percent in 1971. For a high-income family, such costs represented the same share of income (5 percent) in 1999 as in 1971 (College Board, 2000).

Calculating the net price of college—price of attendance minus student aid awards—does not change this picture. Figure 3.2 factors in both student aid awards and families' ability to pay. The results show that the burden—the unmet need—is greatest for lower- and moderate-income families (U.S. Department of Education, 1998). Financial aid, in other words, has not offset the real increases in sticker price over the past two decades.

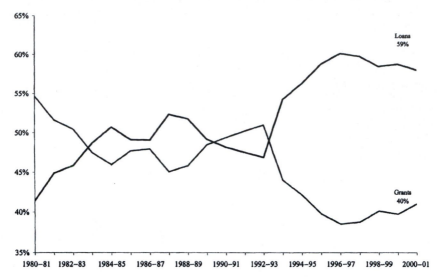

*Figure 3.3 Share of Grants versus Loans, 1980–1981 to 1999–2000*

Source: College Board (2001).

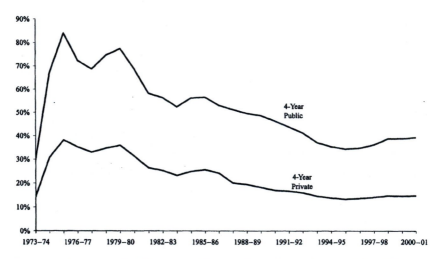

*Figure 3.4 Maximum Pell Grant as a Share of Cost of Attendance, 1973–1974 to 2002–2001*

Source: College Board (2001).

Moreover, the aid these students are receiving increasingly comes in the form of borrowing. Over the past two decades, as reflected in Figure 3.3, student aid has drifted from a grant-based to a loan-based system. Twenty years ago, grants accounted for 55 percent and loans 41 percent of available aid. Ten years ago, the proportions of grant and loan aid were about even. Today loans account for almost 60 percent of the total (College Board, 2001).

In 1999, federally sponsored programs generated more than $36 billion in student and parent loans, five times the size of the Pell Grant program that was meant to be the system's foundation, serving students with the greatest need. As shown in Figure 3.4, since the late 1970s the maximum Pell Grant has dwindled relative to the costs of higher education. Recent increases in Pell Grant appropriations have helped to stabilize the overall balance of aid in the system. Yet the maximum Pell Grant, at $3,300 in 2000, remained far below the purchasing power it had two decades ago. The current maximum covers less than 40 percent of the average fixed costs (tuition and fees, room and board) at a four-year public college, and 15 percent at a private four-year college.

Even those students who are most at risk increasingly must borrow to gain postsecondary access. Table 3.1 indicates that more than two-thirds of lower-income bachelor's degree recipients used loans to offset college costs, compared to one-fourth of those from upper-income backgrounds. And the lower-income student's debt burden is about $3,000 higher on average than that of the upper-income student.

Effects of the shift from grants to loans for financing the cost of college are difficult to ascertain, but the prospect of debt likely discourages many less-advantaged young people from considering postsecondary education. Evidence also indicates that financial assistance in the form of loans is less effective than grant aid in helping students to stay in college and get their degrees (U.S. General Accounting Office, 1995).

Not only has the financial aid system gravitated toward loans, but also the focus of federal policy has evolved from helping students who "but for such aid" would not be able to attend college, to relieving the burden for those who likely would go to college without such support. This shift is reflected most dramatically in the $40 billion of tuition tax benefits enacted as part of the Taxpayer Relief Act of 1997, the Hope and Lifetime Learning Tax Credits, which primarily benefit middle- and upper-middle-income students  (see later in this chapter for more on federal tax credits).

Likewise, many state governments are enacting tuition tax credits and deductions, and they are investing more heavily in merit scholarships as well as college savings and pre-paid plans oriented to middle- and upper-

Table 3.1

Percentage of B.A. Recipients with Federal Student Loan Debt and Average Amount Borrowed, by Family Income, 1995–1996

| Family Income | Public Four-Year | | Private Four-Year | | All Students |
|---|---|---|---|---|---|
| | Percent Borrowing | Ave. Amount Borrowed | Percent Borrowing | Ave. Amount Borrowed | Distribution of B.A. Recipients Who Borrowed |
| Less than $30,000 | 66% | $12,550 | 70% | $15,240 | 45% |
| $30,0000 to $49,999 | 56 | 12,370 | 62 | 13,790 | 18 |
| $50,000 to $69,999 | 40 | 10,320 | 42 | 13,500 | 16 |
| $70,000 or more | 24 | 9,290 | 29 | 12,360 | 21 |
| All Income Levels | 52 | 11,950 | 54 | 14,290 | 100 |

Source: U.S. Department of Education (1997b)

income families (Chapter 4). Furthermore, colleges themselves have increasingly turned to merit-based aid and preferential packaging unrelated to financial need (Chapter 5).

## PERCEPTIONS AND POLITICS

The manner in which college affordability has been covered in the media and framed politically has contributed to the problem. Research by the American Council on Education indicates that most students and families overestimate college prices, on the one hand, and underestimate the availability of financial aid, on the other—in both cases by a wide margin (Ikenberry & Hartle, 1998). In addition, lower-income families are more likely to overestimate the cost of college than are wealthier families. Perceived barriers can be as effective as real ones. Such misapprehensions undoubtedly deter some Americans from pursuing a postsecondary education.

The media have helped to create these misperceptions by narrowly focusing coverage on the highest-priced, elite institutions. Polls have told politicians that the cost of college is near the top of voters' concerns (Immerwahr, 1998). Steadily rising college prices, and the accompanying drumbeat in the media and the political arena, have created a generalized sense of crisis about paying for college. As a result, college affordability has increasingly been defined as an issue for middle- and upper-income students, those most likely and financially able to attend college in the first place. It is to those groups that new incentives, subsidies, and cost relief are primarily being directed.

## TUITION TAX BENEFITS VERSUS DIRECT STUDENT AID

As a result of the Taxpayer Relief Act of 1997, the federal government now has two ways of delivering college financial assistance: through the tax code and through direct appropriations. These two sets of benefits operate on different principles and serve different, although overlapping, populations. Under the tax code, the more income one has (up to the income ceilings established in the law), the more one benefits. Under the need-based aid programs authorized by Title IV of the Higher Education Act, the less income one has, the more one benefits. Tuition tax benefits go primarily to students and families with incomes above the median, whereas most Title IV assistance goes to families below the median.

Over the long haul, how will these two sets of benefits interact? Which will predominate? How will the federal government deliver the bulk of its assistance to students and families for paying postsecondary costs—through the tax code or through Title IV of the Higher Education Act?

Although recent funding increases for Pell Grants have restored some of the buying power lost in this program since the 1970s, there is a long way to go. Like other discretionary (non-entitlement) programs in the federal budget, Pell Grants have no guaranteed financing from year to year. By contrast, the tuition tax breaks function, in effect, as an entitlement that is not tied to annual appropriations. History suggests that once such benefits are written into the tax code, there will be persistent pressure over time to expand eligibility for them, and little political will to eliminate them.

Former president Bill Clinton, under whose administration the Taxpayer Relief Act of 1997 was passed, argued consistently that the country needed to invest more in education and training to boost economic growth, expand opportunity, and reduce income disparities. But tuition tax breaks are not an effective means to achieve these worthy objectives. They are one way to cut taxes, but not a sound strategy for lifting the country's net investment in education or eliminating discrepancies in opportunity.

Looking ahead ten to fifteen years, tuition tax relief is certainly not the best way to ensure opportunity for the coming tidal wave of college-age students that will be more diverse and divided economically than any previous generation in our country (Chapter 8). Such federal funding would be better invested in Pell Grants and other need-based student assistance under the Higher Education Act.

## REASSERTING FEDERAL LEADERSHIP

The Higher Education Act of 1965 called for a partnership between the federal government and the campuses in widening access to college. The original legislation established Educational Opportunity Grants (EOG), the first explicit federal commitment to equalizing college opportunities for students regardless of ability to pay. The EOGs were to go to students who "but for such aid" would not be able to attend college, and colleges seeking an allocation under this new program were required to make "vigorous" efforts to identify and recruit students with "exceptional financial need." In 1972 Congress created the Basic Educational Opportunity Grant, later renamed for its chief sponsor Senator Claiborne Pell, and the original EOG program was renamed Supplemental Opportunity Grants. The

1972 law also established federal matching funds for states that invested in need-based grants, through the State Student Incentive Grant program, thus rounding out a federal-state-institutional partnership.

Today we need to summon a renewed spirit of partnership in order to expand opportunity and meet our society's need for a skilled and competitive workforce. Financial aid remains as important now as when the Higher Education Act was passed in 1965—that is, aid that is targeted to students with the fewest resources and delivered to students and families as simply and predictably as possible.

The single most important thing the federal government could do to redeem its commitment to equality of opportunity is to restore the promise and purchasing power that Pell Grants once represented for lower-income students. The constant-dollar value of the maximum Pell Grant was at its peak in the middle to late 1970s. Based on changes in cost of attendance since then, restoring the value of Pell would require a maximum grant in the range of $7,000 to $8,000, which would in turn require a $12 to $15 billion boost in appropriations (Figure 3.5).

I realize that these numbers are far outside the frame of reference of current budget discussions, which tend to focus on relatively small and incremental increases in funding for existing programs. But this is what it would take to make Pell Grants the powerful engine for lower-income students that they were intended to be. In addition, the more dollars invested in Pell Grants, the more help the program is able to offer not only to the neediest students but also to moderate-income students who are now just out of range of eligibility for the awards.

While Pell Grants compete for annual appropriations, tuition breaks written into the tax code amount to a new entitlement for middle- and upper-income citizens. Real increases in Pell Grant funding will not come easily under prevailing budget rules and politics, and neither will the idea of creating a new entitlement program. However, in fairness and in anticipation of the coming tidal wave of students, a Pell Grant entitlement is what we ought to have.

If tuition tax relief will not close the opportunity gap, neither will the Bush administration's proposal to boost state merit scholarship programs. Federal incentives to states to create and expand merit scholarships would be redundant, since most of the states are already doing this, and such federal outlays would contribute little to assuring access for lower- and moderate-income students. Resources the Bush administration proposes to invest in merit scholarships would be better directed to Pell Grants and other need-based aid under Title IV of the Higher Education Act.

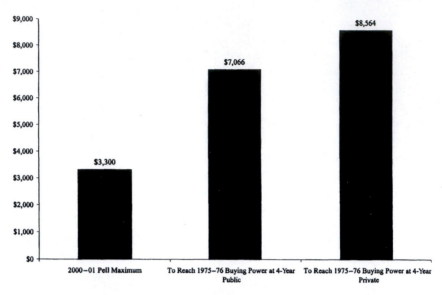

*Figure 3.5 Returning Buying Power to the Pell Grant*

*Source*: Author's calculations.

## FINANCIAL AID IS NOT ENOUGH

Finally, it is important to remind ourselves that financial aid is a necessary but insufficient condition for equalizing the chance to attend and complete college. Access is not enough, nor is financial aid. The problem of unequal opportunity has proved more intractable than anyone anticipated in the early years of the Higher Education Act. This is to say not that aid programs have failed but, rather, that too much may have been expected of them. Complementary approaches, including early intervention and collateral support services, are obviously required (Chapters 6 and 7).

Above all, we need a much wider and deeper societal commitment to reaching, motivating, and preparing at-risk students for college—and assuring that cost is not a barrier.

## NOTE

1. All years shown refer to the fall of each academic year; that is, 1979 is academic year 1979–1980.

# REFERENCES

College Board. (2000). *Trends in college pricing, 2000*. New York: Author.

College Board. (2001). *Trends in student aid, 2001*. New York: Author.

Halperin, S. M. (ed.). (1998). *The forgotten half revisited*. Washington, DC: American Youth Policy Forum.

Ikenberry, S. O., & Hartle, T. W. (1998). *Too little knowledge is a dangerous thing: What the public thinks about paying for college*. Washington, DC: American Council on Education.

Immerwahr, J. (1998). *The price of admission: The growing importance of higher education*. San Jose, CA: National Center for Public Policy and Higher Education.

U.S. Bureau of the Census. (2000). *Money income in the United States: 1999* (P60-209). Washington, DC: Author.

U.S. Department of Education, National Center for Education Statistics. (1997a). *Access to postsecondary education for 1992 high school graduates*. Washington, DC: Author.

U.S. Department of Education, National Center for Education Statistics. (1997b). *National postsecondary student aid study, 1995–96*. Washington, DC: NCES.

U.S. Department of Education, National Center for Education Statistics. (1998). *The condition of education, 1998*. Washington, DC: Author.

U.S. Department of Education, National Center for Education Statistics. (2001). *Digest of education statistics, 2000*. Washington, DC: Author.

U.S. General Accounting Office. (1995). *Higher education: Restructuring student aid could reduce low-income student dropout rate* (GAO/HEHS-95-48). Washington, DC: Author.

# CHAPTER 4

# State Aid and Student Access: The Changing Picture

## Donald E. Heller

T he states have long played an important role in subsidizing higher education in this country, along with the federal government, colleges and universities themselves, and private sources. Slightly over one-third of the costs of higher education are provided by states in the form of direct appropriations to public colleges and universities and financial aid to students. Although support through their appropriations is much the larger share, direct state aid to students is important nonetheless.[1]

The College Board conducts an annual survey of the financial aid dollars available to undergraduate and graduate students combined. The latest survey found that state-funded grants and loans totaled approximately $4.1 billion (6 percent) of the $68 billion in aid awarded in the 1999–2000 academic year (College Board, 2000). The role of state financial aid in subsidizing undergraduate education, however, is likely greater than these figures imply. While the board does not distinguish between aid awarded to undergraduates versus graduate students, the great majority of state grants—over 97 percent, according to the most recent report of the National Association of State Student Grant and Aid Programs (2002)—is awarded to undergraduate students. This exceeds the proportion awarded to undergraduates by many of the other sources.

The states' importance in ensuring access to and affordability of higher education was underscored in a report issued by the National Center for Public Policy and Higher Education (2000). Governor James B. Hunt of North Carolina, chair of the Board of Directors of the center, stated in the report that "[t]he emphasis here is on states because in the American system the states bear primary responsibility for higher education policy and for support of higher education. States also play an important role in providing financial assistance to students in public and private higher education" (p. 9). The wide range of performance by the states in upholding this responsibility was noted in the report: "Despite the accomplishments of American higher education, its benefits are unevenly and often unfairly distributed, and do not reflect the distribution of talent in American society. Geography, wealth, income, and ethnicity still play far too great a role in determining the educational opportunities and life chances of Americans" (p. 10).

This chapter examines the role of state financial assistance in promoting access to undergraduate education in the nation. A brief history of state support for higher education highlights the interaction between direct state subsidy of institutions and targeted student grants. We review recent trends in state student aid policies, with an emphasis on the shift from need-based to merit-based awards and the implications of this change for students from low-income families. The final section draws conclusions and raises questions for further deliberation.

## HISTORY OF STATE SUPPORT FOR HIGHER EDUCATION

### State Support and Financial Aid[2]

State support for higher education in the United States began with allocations to private, largely church-chartered institutions, often in the form of public land grants and state-authorized lotteries set up to benefit the schools. In the late eighteenth and early nineteenth centuries states began to provide direct funding for private colleges and universities from general tax revenues. The first truly "public" institutions of higher education were chartered in the late eighteenth century, primarily in the South and Midwest. These institutions received direct state subsidy, although their control can best be described as "quasi-public" because of the degree of autonomy generally granted to their trustees.

The most important event in the expansion of state support for higher education was the passage of the Morrill Act in 1862. Sponsored by Representative Justin Morrill of Vermont, the act provided federal land grants to states that created colleges and universities "to teach such branches of learning as are related to agriculture and the mechanic arts" (quoted in Rudolph, 1990, p. 252). The states were permitted to sell the land and turn over the proceeds to the colleges. The Morrill Act encouraged the founding of many public colleges and universities, all funded primarily through direct state appropriations.

These early public colleges and universities generally charged very low tuition, thus promoting affordability for all. Even so, some recognized that charging *any* tuition at public institutions could effectively prevent certain students from attending. A number of schools did provide very limited scholarships to some of their neediest students, but these programs were not core to the mission of the institutions and often came and went.

Public college tuition began to rise in the twentieth century; student fees that made up 12 percent of operating revenues in 1927 had grown to 20 percent of receipts by 1940. Although still inexpensive compared to private colleges, tuition at public universities continued to increase in the post–World War II era. The rise was at least partially enabled by the GI Bill, which provided generous tuition scholarships to veterans that more than covered the cost of attendance at a public institution. Following the war, President Harry Truman appointed a commission to examine higher education. The final report of the President's Commission on Higher Education (1947) raised a number of concerns regarding access to postsecondary education for the country's neediest students. A primary recommendation of the commission was the creation of federal need-based aid programs, but it also recognized the obligation of states to protect the interests of students from low-income families. "Irrespective of, and in addition to whatever program of grants-in-aid the Federal Government may decide to adopt, this Commission urges generous extension of State scholarship provisions" (Vol. 2, p. 47).

Almost two decades passed before the federal government acted on the commission's recommendation and authorized broad-based college aid programs through the Higher Education Act of 1965 (HEA). Although some states had started their own scholarship programs by this time, these contributed a very small amount to the total dollars awarded to students. The first reauthorization of the HEA in 1972 created the important State Student Incentive Grant (SSIG) program, which provided federal matching funds for state-run, need-based grants. This program proved critical to the development and expansion of the state aid initiatives. In 1969, nineteen states appropriated just under $200 million for state-funded grants; by 1974 this support had expanded to thirty-six states and totaled $423 million (Fenske & Boyd, 1981). By 1979, every state and the District of Columbia reported at least one grant program, and the total appropriated reached over $800 million (National Association of State Scholarship and Grant Programs, various years). A 1975 survey commented that "[g]rowth represented in '74–75 and '75–76 to a large degree, is a response to the new

SSIG Program which permits up to a $1,500 annual student award (equal shares of $750 Federal/State) in this new form of State/Federal partnership" (Boyd, 1975, p. 2).

Although the SSIG program (renamed the Leveraging Educational Assistance Partnership—LEAP—Program in the 1990s) may have spurred the development of state scholarship programs, it is difficult to credit it for their entire subsequent growth. In its first year of operation (academic year 1974–1975), the program distributed $19 million, a small portion of the $423 million spent by the states on student aid that year. Whereas state grant appropriations grew almost 750 percent from 1974 to 1998, funding for the SSIG program topped out at $78 million in 1981, an increase of just over 300 percent (College Board, 2000). Annual funding for SSIG/LEAP stayed in the range of $60 to $70 million through most of the 1980s and 1990s, before being cut back to $25 million in 1998. Despite annual attempts by the Clinton administration to kill the program, Congress has kept it on fiscal life support.

## Tuition Prices and State Support since the 1960s

Since the 1960s, two trends have dominated the financing of public higher education. First, tuition has increased faster than both the general inflation rate and income growth across the country. Additionally, state support for higher education (in the form of appropriations and state aid) has fallen as a share of total state expenditures and has not kept pace with enrollment growth in public institutions. The net effect of these two trends—increasing tuition costs and stagnating levels of state support—has been an important shift in the burden of financing public higher education. Figure 4.1 shows taxpayer support for public institutions of higher learning (in the form of state appropriations and state scholarship programs) versus expenditures by students and their families (tuition and fees).[3] In 1969, the states provided 60 percent of the expenditures, and tuition and fees provided 15 percent. By 1978, the difference between these shares had widened to over 47 percent, largely because of the increasing state support during this period and the decrease in real tuition costs in the mid-1970s. From 1978 on, the difference narrowed as tuition increased and state support diminished. In 1995 students and their families were shouldering 23 percent of expenditures, and state support had dropped to 47 percent. The difference of 24 percent was little more than half the level of 1978.

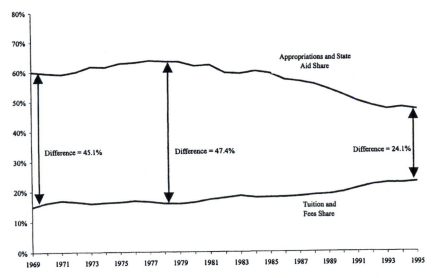

*Figure 4.1 State Support and Student Fees as Shares of Expenditures for Public Colleges and Universities, 1969–1995*

Source: Author's calculations from NASSGP (various years) and Quantum Research Corporation (2001).

## RECENT TRENDS IN STATE FINANCIAL AID FUNDING

Unlike overall state spending on higher education, funding for state undergraduate grant programs has increased fourfold in real dollars over the last three decades. Figure 4.2 shows the increases in current and constant (1998) dollars. Since 1969, real spending (after inflation) has increased at an annual rate of 5 percent. When first developed, most of these state grant programs mirrored the goal of the federal Title IV programs in the Higher Education Act of 1965—that of providing financial assistance to needy students (see Chapter 1). As described by Fenske and Boyd (1981), "Access and choice are two principal themes in student aid that have become familiar through frequent and thorough discussion over the past 20 years as they unfolded first in hortatory statements, then in large and growing funded student aid programs" (p. 2). The original commitment to promoting access held steady throughout the 1970s and 1980s, with financial need as the primary criterion for the awarding of scholarships. Of the eighty-four undergraduate state grant programs surveyed in 1980–1981 by the National Association of State Scholarship and Grant Programs, forty-four used exclusively financial need-based criteria, one used exclusively merit criteria, twenty-nine used measures of both financial need and merit,

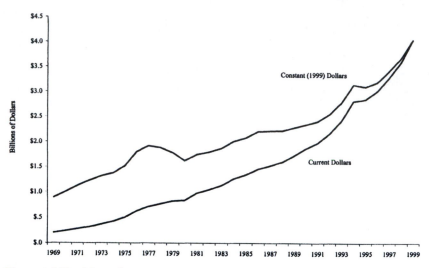

*Figure 4.2 Total State Grant Appropriations for Undergraduates, 1969–1999*

Source: Author's calculations from Fenske and Boyd (1981); NASSGP (various years); and National Center for Education Statistics (2000, Table 38).

and ten were unclassifiable from the information provided (National Association of State Scholarship and Grant Programs, various years). The great majority of the grant awards, therefore, took financial need into account. Varying criteria were used by states to determine academic achievement or merit, including high school or college grade point average, class rank, Scholastic Aptitude Test (SAT) or American College Test (ACT) scores, and recommendations.

In the academic year 1981–82, the National Association of State Scholarship and Grant Programs began to more systematically track the higher education aid programs that did *not* use financial need as a criterion for selection (National Association of State Scholarship and Grant Programs, various years). Many of these programs were targeted to specific populations, such as the children of deceased or permanently disabled firefighters or law enforcement officers (Delaware, Georgia, Idaho, Massachusetts, New Jersey); descendants of Confederate soldiers and sailors (Florida); and children of deceased or disabled war veterans (Florida, Massachusetts). Most of these special programs were very small, awarding fewer than 100 scholarships annually. Other programs, which generally served many more students, did award scholarships based on academic merit. The 1981–1982 survey found that 60.3 percent of awards to undergraduates were based on need alone; 30.7 percent were based on a combination of financial need and non-need criteria; and 9.0 percent were based on non-need criteria alone.

Over the next dozen years, both need- and non-need-based programs grew substantially and at similar rates, keeping the proportion of the award dollars at approximately the same levels. Whereas the total dollars awarded to undergraduates grew from $975 million in 1981–1982 to $2.4 billion in 1993–1994, the percentage of dollars awarded without using financial need as a measure fluctuated between 8.9 percent and 11.1 percent of the total.

A turning point in the structure and funding of the state financial aid programs came in 1993, when Governor Zell Miller created the Georgia Helping Outstanding Pupils Educationally (HOPE) Scholarship program. The program kicked off an expansion in merit aid programs nationally, as shown in Figure 4.3.

Since 1993, undergraduate state aid programs have shifted away from the steady and proportional growth of need- and non-need-based grants toward awards based on merit. In the sixteen years since the National Association of State Scholarship and Grant Programs began to track merit programs separately, funding for them has increased 336 percent in real dollars, whereas funding for the need-based programs has increased only 88 percent. In 1982, the share of dollars in the merit programs was 9.3 percent of the total appropriated by the states; by 1999, this share had increased to 22 percent.

## THE IMPLICATIONS OF THE SHIFT TOWARD MERIT AID

Although over 75 percent of all undergraduate state grant awards are still based on financial need, the emphasis in recent years has been on the establishment and expansion of merit-based programs. The Georgia HOPE program—the first broad-based merit program introduced by a state—was followed by similar programs in Arkansas, Kentucky, Florida, Louisiana, Michigan, Nevada, New Mexico, and West Virginia as states jumped on the bandwagon in an attempt to cash in on the political popularity of these scholarships. Like Georgia's, most of these programs use no means testing whatsoever; the children of the rich are as eligible for the scholarships as are the children of the poor.

Chapter 1 of this volume discusses the gap in college attendance between students from low- and upper-income families. Although poverty is not the only barrier to college entry, research has amply documented the importance of financial aid in promoting postsecondary education for economically disadvantaged students (see Heller, 1997; Jackson & Weath-

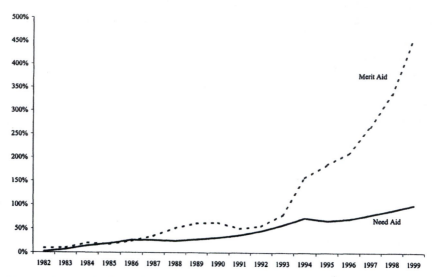

*Figure 4.3 Growth of State Need-based and Merit Aid in Constant Dollars, 1982–1999*

Source: Author's calculations from NASSGP (various years).

ersby, 1975; and Leslie & Brinkman, 1987, for reviews of the college access literature over the last three decades).

Besides the lack of means testing, other aspects of many of the state-funded merit scholarship programs are also troubling, especially when examined against the background of their original access-promoting mission. Many of the programs, including those in Georgia, Florida, Kentucky, and New Mexico, are funded from state lottery revenues. A study of state lotteries by economists Charles Clotfelter and Philip Cook (1991) concluded, "[T]he evidence is quite clear that the implicit lottery tax is decidedly regressive. That is to say, an increase in the revenue from lotteries has exactly the same distributional impact as the imposition of or increase in a similarly regressive tax" (p. 227). Regressive taxes impose a proportionally lower tax burden as income rises; therefore, lower-income taxpayers pay a greater percentage of their income than do higher-income taxpayers. Since many of these scholarships go to students from upper-middle and high-income families, these policies promote what one report described as "a popular wealth transfer from low- and mid-income people to the well-to-do" ("A not very bright idea" 1997, p. 2D). Cook noted the irony of funding scholarships by means of lottery revenues: "An education lottery is an odd link between two government enterprises. One exploits the public ignorance, and the other is supposed to be helping that ignorance" (Selingo, 1999, p. A38).

Some less-publicized issues are equally, if not more, disturbing. For example, until recently the Georgia HOPE program required that students use federal Pell Grants as a source of financial aid *before* they could be awarded the tuition and fee payments allowed under HOPE. Because tuition and fees in public institutions in Georgia have been below the Pell Grant maximum since HOPE was created, HOPE dollars could not be used to pay for other costs of attendance such as room, board, and travel expenses. Thus, the lowest-income Georgians (those eligible for the maximum Pell Grant from the federal government) received nothing from HOPE other than the book allowance (currently $300 per year). This has resulted in a program that Patrick Callan claims "was structured to exclude the participation of low-income students who received federal Pell Grants, a kind of reverse means testing" (Callan, 2001, p. 88).[4]

Little research has examined the socioeconomic status of the students who are awarded these merit scholarships.[5] The available evidence, however, indicates that many of these programs "give subsidies to students who are already college bound" (Callan, 2001, p. 88). A recent Florida study examined the family incomes of students who were awarded the state's Bright Futures Merit Scholarships in the 1998–1999 academic year. Twenty-nine percent of the scholarships went to students from families making more than $70,000 a year, and 11.5 percent to those from families making more than $100,000 a year. Only 37 percent of the scholarships were awarded to students from families with an annual income of less than $40,000; in comparison 95 percent of all Pell Grants are awarded to students from families making below $40,000 (U.S. Department of Education, 2000; Postsecondary Education Planning Committee, 1999). In Louisiana, the Office of Student Financial Assistance found that 15 percent of students awarded the state's Tuition Opportunity Program for Students (TOPS) Merit Scholarships in the 1999–2000 school year went to students from families with incomes of at least $100,000 (Dyer, 2000).

The 1999 Florida report also found that Bright Futures scholarships were awarded disproportionately to white and Asian American students. For example, whereas whites and Asian Americans in Florida represented 65 percent of all public high school graduates, they were awarded 81 percent of the scholarships. African Americans and Hispanics, who together represented over one-third of high school graduates, were awarded only 17 percent of the scholarships. It has been well documented that the college participation rates of African Americans and Hispanics in this country continue to lag behind those of whites and Asian Americans (Heller, 1999).

Another recent study looked at the first cohort of students eligible for the Michigan Merit Award Scholarships, a newly implemented program funded from the state's share of the national tobacco lawsuit settlement. The authorizing legislation established as one of the program's two goals the expansion of access to higher education in the state, but examination showed similar levels of racial disparity as in the Florida program. White and Asian American students, who represented 72 percent of students who took the tests necessary to qualify for the scholarships, won 91 percent of the awards. African Americans and Hispanics, who together represented 22 percent of the test-taking pool, were awarded fewer than 5 percent of the scholarships. The study also examined the wealth of the school districts of the eligible awardees; it found that a disproportionate share of Michigan's merit scholarships went to students in the state's wealthiest school districts. The authors concluded that the "scholarships will be awarded disproportionately to those students who are most likely to be attending college anyway, even without the grant assistance ... Whites, Asian Americans, and students in wealthier school districts" (Heller & Shapiro, 2000, p. 20).

The uneven distribution of awards in the Michigan program has led to a "disparate impact," in legal parlance. This is the core allegation in a federal lawsuit filed against the Michigan program in June 2000 by a coalition of groups headed by the American Civil Liberties Union of Michigan. The suit, *White et al. v. Engler et al.*, alleges that the program violates the civil rights of minority and economically disadvantaged students through the use of scholarship award criteria that are not educationally defensible.

A similar suit was filed in federal court in Arkansas, alleging that a merit scholarship program in that state discriminates against minority students. Since 1997, the Arkansas Governor's Distinguished Scholar program has given only 4 of the 808 grants (less than one-half of 1 percent) to African Americans, in a state where approximately 20 percent of the high school graduates are African Americans (Minton & Courage, 2000).

It cannot be determined whether the funding for the merit scholarships comes at the expense of need-based aid, or whether it represents a new infusion of funds to state scholarship programs. In other words, is every dollar budgeted for merit scholarship programs a dollar that would otherwise be spent on need-based aid? Or does it represent a dollar that would have been spent on other state priorities? Although the answer is not known, it is evident that the purposes and goals of the merit programs are out of sync with the historical emphasis of state grant programs on increasing college access for the neediest students. A 1997 news item contained a vignette that sums up the frustration of Charles Reed, former chancellor of the state

university system in Florida, with the Bright Futures program and merit
scholarships in general:

> A man approached Chancellor Charles Reed in Miami recently to tell him
> what a wonderful university system Florida has. Reed asked him to explain.
> The man said his two children at the University of Florida were receiving
> new lottery-funded scholarships. But Reed was troubled when he learned
> that the man was an orthopedic surgeon who could easily afford university
> tuition without financial aid from the state. "Something is really wrong when
> you do that," Reed said.... "When you can give something away to the mid-
> dle and upper-middle class, in politics, it doesn't get any better than that"
> (Dunkelberger, 1997, p. 1A).

## CONCLUSION

The trend toward state-funded merit scholarships is well established and
shows little sign of abating.[6] As Reed and others have described, these programs are extremely popular with voters, especially middle- and upper-income families who do not generally benefit from need-based grant programs. This shift has helped to refocus the purpose of state financial aid
away from the goal of ensuring equality of educational opportunity toward
rewarding whatever qualities each state has established as determining
"merit." Definitions of merit vary from state to state: In Georgia, it is
achieving a B average in academic track courses in high school and maintaining that average in college. Florida and Louisiana require a minimum
grade point average in high school in combination with a range of standardized test scores. In New Mexico, it is achieving a 2.5 grade point average in college, and Michigan students must score above an established
level on all four of the eleventh grade statewide tests.

Academic merit is clearly not the only criteria at play in these programs,
however. As Governor John Engler of Michigan described it in his 1999
State of the State address, "Our Michigan Merit Award will make college
more affordable and will reward achievement and hard work" (Engler,
1999). Yet neither the governor nor other state officials have presented
any evidence that students who qualify for these scholarships do, in fact,
work hard. William G. Bowen and Derek Bok point out: "It is not clear
that students who receive higher grades and test scores have necessarily
worked harder in school. Grades and test scores are a reflection not only
of effort but of intelligence, family circumstances, and early upbringing,
that have nothing to do with how many hours students have labored over
their homework" (Bowen & Bok, 2000, p. 277).

Although encouraging students to "work hard" or achieve more in high school may be laudable goals for states, policymakers need to understand how merit aid programs affect students from low-income families. If the criteria for awarding the scholarships can be established in a manner that targets the financially neediest students, then states may be able to accomplish these "merit" goals in concert with promoting educational opportunity and equity. However, if merit programs end up distributing their rewards to students who are likely to attend college anyway, as the initial evidence suggests, then the states will be backing away from their commitment to enable educational opportunity for needy students. Thomas Mortenson, a long-time observer of financial aid policy in the nation, has summed up this idea perhaps as well as anybody:

> In the economic world of highly constrained social welfare maximization, giving scarce financial aid resources to people who do not need them is wasteful, unnecessary, unproductive, and comes at the price of adequate and appropriate student financial aid for others who could not afford to attend college without such assistance. (Mortenson, 1997, p. 2)

## NOTES

1. Little data are available on private scholarship assistance, which includes local organizations such as Rotary Clubs as well as groups such as Citizens' Scholarship Foundation of America (parent organization of the many Dollars for Scholars programs throughout the country).

2. This section is adapted from Heller (2002).

3. It should be noted that a portion of the tuition and fees paid by students and their families is covered by federal Pell Grants and other non-state financial aid. Even if these other sources are subtracted from gross tuition and fees, the shift in the funding pattern over time is pronounced. One can still argue that this funding pattern represents a shift of the burden from the state to students, with students paying for college from their own earnings and savings, contributions from parents, and financial aid from non-state sources.

4. In March 2000 the Georgia legislature passed a bill correcting this inequity. The bill allows HOPE recipients to use their award to pay for tuition and fees, and to use Pell dollars to pay for room, board, and other expenses, thus increasing the total amount of grants (state and federal combined) for which low-income students are eligible.

5. Most of the state need-based scholarship programs use the same methodology used by the federal Title IV programs to determine award eligibility.

6. The 2000 California legislation to triple the funding for the Cal Grant program to over $1 billion annually by 2006 is a welcome exception to this trend. Al-

though the Cal Grant program has a merit component, it also has fairly stringent income requirements and it awards the majority of its dollars to students in lower- and lower-middle-income families.

# REFERENCES

Bowen, W.G., & Bok, D. (2000). *The shape of the river: Long-term consequences of considering race in college and university admissions.* Princeton, N.J.: Princeton University Press.

Boyd, J.D. (1975). *State/territory funded scholarship/grant programs to undergraduate students with financial need to attend public or private post-secondary educational institutions. 7th annual survey, 1975–76 academic year.* Deerfield: Illinois State Scholarship Commission.

Callan, P.M. (2001). Reframing access and opportunity: Problematic state and federal higher education policy in the 1990s. In D.E. Heller (ed.), *The states and public higher education policy: Affordability, access, and accountability.* Baltimore: Johns Hopkins University Press.

Clotfelter, C.T., & Cook, P.J. (1991). *Selling hope: State lotteries in America.* Cambridge, MA: Harvard University Press.

College Board. (2000). *Trends in student aid 2000.* Washington, DC: Author.

Dunkelberger, L. (1997, December 20). "Bright futures" dim for poor; the scholarships tend to benefit middle- and upper-income students, critics say. *Sarasota Herald-Tribune,* p. 1A.

Dyer, S. (2000, August 1). 15 percent of TOPS recipients from upper-income families. *The Advocate,* p. 10A.

Engler, J. (1999, January 28). *1999 state of the state address: Michigan the "smart state," first in the 21st century.* (http://www.state.mi.us/migov/gov/Speeches / StateoftheState_1999.html). Lansing, MI: Office of the Governor.

Fenske, R.H., & Boyd, J.D. (1981). *State need-based college scholarship and grant programs: A study of their development, 1969–1980.* New York: College Entrance Examination Board.

Heller, D.E. (1997). Student price response in higher education: An update to Leslie and Brinkman. *Journal of Higher Education, 68*(6), 624–59.

Heller, D.E. (1999). Racial equity in college participation: African American students in the United States. *Review of African American Education, 1*(1), 5–29.

Heller, D.E. (2002). The policy shift in state financial aid programs. In J.C. Smart (ed.), *Higher education: Handbook of theory and research, Vol. XVII.* New York: Agathon Press.

Heller, D.E., & Shapiro, D.T. (2000, November). High-stakes testing and state financial aid: Evidence from Michigan. Paper presented at the annual conference of the Association for the Study of Higher Education, Sacramento, CA.

Jackson, G. A., & Weathersby, G. B. (1975). Individual demand for higher education. *Journal of Higher Education, 46*(6), 623–52.

Leslie, L. L., & Brinkman, P. T. (1987). Student price response in higher education. *Journal of Higher Education, 58*(2): 181–204.

Minton, M., & Courage, T. (2000, September 7). Challenging scholarships, two atop class sue, cite bias. *Arkansas Democrat-Gazette*, p. B1.

Mortenson, T. G. (1997). Georgia's HOPE Scholarship program: Good intentions, strong funding, bad design. *Postsecondary Education Opportunity, 56*(February), 1–3.

National Association of State Scholarship and Grant Programs/National Association of State Student Grant and Aid Programs. (Various years). *NASSGP/NASSGAP annual survey report*. Deerfield: Illinois State Scholarship Commission; Harrisburg: Pennsylvania Higher Education Assistance Agency; and Albany: New York State Higher Education Services Corporation.

National Center for Education Statistics. (2000). *Digest of education statistics, 1999*. Washington, DC: U.S. Department of Education.

National Center for Public Policy and Higher Education (2000). *Measuring up 2000: The state-by-state report card for higher education*. San Jose, CA: Author.

A not very bright idea. (1997, December 21). *St. Petersburg Times*, p. 2D.

Postsecondary Education Planning Commission. (1999). *Florida's Bright Futures Scholarship Program: A baseline evaluation*. Tallahassee, FL: Author.

President's Commission on Higher Education. (1947). *Higher education for American democracy*. New York: Harper & Brothers.

Quantum Research Corporation. (2001). *CASPAR database system*. http://caspar.nsf.gov. Bethesda, MD: Author.

Rudolph, F. (1990). *The American college and university: A history*. (1990 ed.). Athens: University of Georgia Press.

Selingo, J. (1999, April 16). Seeking dollars to further their dreams, scholarship supporters push for lotteries. *Chronicle of Higher Education*, p. A38.

U.S. Department of Education, Office of Postsecondary Education. (2000). *Title IV/Federal Pell Grant program 1998–99 end of year report*. Washington, DC: Author.

# CHAPTER 5

# Changing Patterns of Institutional Aid: Impact on Access and Education Policy

*Michael S. McPherson and Morton Owen Schapiro*

Resources to help lower-income families defray the costs of higher education and provide meaningful postsecondary choices for their children have dwindled over the past few decades. Both state and federal governments have decreased their levels of grants and loans targeted exclusively to economically disadvantaged students and their families, and there is reason to believe that this trend will continue (see Chapters 3 and 4). Colleges and universities have also shifted their practices in providing student aid—both need based and merit based—to target more benefits to middle- and upper-income students. This chapter examines the incentives underlying these changes in institutional aid and assesses their impact within the context of already constricted educational resources. Our analysis points to the growing disparity between our shared national ideal of equity in educational opportunity and the policies and practices that increasingly limit access to higher education for lower-income students. Finally, we suggest ways in which institutional, state, and federal financial aid programs could work together to increase access for economically disadvantaged students, and we examine the implications if such action fails to materialize.[1]

## TRENDS IN FINANCING

For twenty years, from the early 1960s to the early 1980s, public resources for the support of higher education grew. Since the mid-1980s on, this

**Table 5.1**

**Share of Higher Education Revenue, by Source, Selected Academic Years, 1939–1996**

| Year | Gross Tuition | Tuition Paid By | | | | Non-tuition Revenue | | |
|---|---|---|---|---|---|---|---|---|
| | | Families | Institutions | Government | | Federal | State & Local | Endowment Earnings |
| | | | | Federal | State | | | |
| 1939-40 | 37% | 35% | 2% | 0% | 0% | 7% | 33% | 21% |
| 1949-50 | 40 | 37 | 3 | 0 | 0 | 12 | 32 | 12 |
| 1959-60 | 26 | 22 | 3 | 0 | 1 | 23 | 34 | 13 |
| 1965-66 | 26 | 21 | 4 | 0 | 1 | 26 | 33 | 9 |
| 1969-70 | 25 | 20 | 4 | 0 | 1 | 22 | 38 | 8 |
| 1975-76 | 26 | 16 | 4 | 4 | 2 | 20 | 43 | 8 |
| 1979-80 | 26 | 14 | 4 | 6 | 2 | 19 | 43 | 9 |
| 1985-86 | 29 | 17 | 5 | 5 | 2 | 16 | 41 | 10 |
| 1989-90 | 31 | 19 | 5 | 5 | 2 | 16 | 37 | 10 |
| 1991-92 | 34 | 22 | 5 | 5 | 2 | 16 | 35 | 10 |
| 1992-93 | 35 | 23 | 5 | 5 | 2 | 16 | 33 | 10 |
| 1993-94 | 35 | 22 | 6 | 5 | 2 | 16 | 32 | 10 |
| 1994-95 | 35 | 23 | 6 | 4 | 2 | 16 | 32 | 10 |
| 1995-96 | 36 | 24 | 6 | 4 | 2 | 15 | 31 | 11 |

*Notes:* 1995–1996 data are preliminary. Figures do not include revenue from auxiliary enterprises or from sales and services. Both veterans' educational benefits and Social Security benefits paid to qualified college students are excluded from federal tuition payments.

*Source:* See McPherson and Schapiro (1991a), p. 23; for data after 1986, see U.S. Department of Education, National Center for Education Statistics (1999), p. 348, Table 324, and the College Board (1998), p. 6, Table 1.

trend has reversed. As the share of college costs financed by the federal and state governments has fallen, the share borne by families has inevitably increased. Tuition is replacing government spending to support operations at both public and private institutions of higher learning.

## Changing Roles of Government Funding

Table 5.1 reports revenue shares by major contributors and also breaks down gross tuition by its sources—the share paid by families directly and the shares paid by various forms of student aid. The most striking trend is the steady decline through 1980 in the share of tuition paid by families. During this period costs of higher education shifted away from families as a result of increased state appropriations to support burgeoning enrollments at state institutions, the growth of federal grants and contracts, and the rise in financial aid available to students and their families. The decline in costs of higher education to families came to an abrupt halt in the 1980s, however, with the family share increasing by 10 percentage points from 1979 to 1995, reaching the highest level—24 percent—since before 1959.[2]

These data show that the role of states in financing higher education has changed more significantly than that of the federal government. As late as 1979, state governments contributed 45 percent of higher education revenues, almost all through direct (non-tuition) support of public institutions. By 1995 that share had fallen to 33 percent. This is true even though states' economic fortunes improved considerably since we first began tracking these numbers in 1990, and the downward trend in the share of higher education revenues provided by the states is so far unabated.

The share of higher education revenues supplied by federal student aid has remained roughly constant since the mid-1970s, but the contribution of federal research support has declined substantially, to 15 percent from its high of 26 percent in the mid-1960s. Since research support is concentrated in a fairly small number of institutions, this decline is of major importance for that subgroup.

## Types of Aid Programs

Changes in patterns of institutional aid are linked to broader trends in resources available directly to students. Table 5.2 shows the overall magnitudes of federal and other forms of student aid for selected years from 1963 to 1999, expressed in constant (1998) dollars. Before 1975, a fairly modest total of generally available aid was divided between guaranteed loans and the so-called campus-based programs, which provide grants, loans, and work-study stipends allocated at the discretion of colleges and universities. From 1975 to 1980, the generally available aid budget doubled in real dollars. Much of this growth was fueled by the newly introduced Basic Educational Opportunity Grant program (later renamed Pell Grants), the means-tested program put in place in the 1972 reauthorization of the Higher Education Act.

From 1980 to the early 1990s, growth in both the Pell program and guaranteed loans increased more slowly, by about one-third each in real dollars. Since 1990, growth in guaranteed and direct loans has been enormous, amounting to a real increase of 116 percent through 1998. During this same period, however, real expenditures in the Pell program rose by only about 20 percent. Thus, although total federal aid increased from $26.1 billion in 1990 to $46.0 billion in 1998, most of this increase was in the form of loans rather than grants.

The real value of state grants has risen throughout the period, but the absolute increase has been dwarfed by the growth in institutional grants, which have increased almost fourfold over the past two decades, from $3.1

Table 5.2

Aid Awarded to Students, by Source, Selected Academic Years, 1963–1998 (in millions of 1998 dollars)

| | 1963–64 | 1970–71 | 1975–76 | 1980–81 | 1985–86 | 1990–91 | 1995–96 | 1997–98 | 1998–99 |
|---|---|---|---|---|---|---|---|---|---|
| **Federal Aid Programs** | | | | | | | | | |
| *Generally available aid* | | | | | | | | | |
| Pell grants | $0 | $0 | $2,745 | $4,530 | $5,435 | $6,059 | $5,822 | $6,435 | $7,242 |
| Supplemental educational opportunity grants | 0 | 681 | 712 | 700 | 622 | 562 | 620 | 593 | 614 |
| State student incentive grants | 0 | 0 | 58 | 137 | 115 | 72 | 68 | 51 | 25 |
| Work study | 0 | 829 | 874 | 1,253 | 991 | 894 | 813 | 921 | 1,002 |
| Perkins loans | 606 | 995 | 1,364 | 1,316 | 1,062 | 1,069 | 1,095 | 1,079 | 1,058 |
| Guaranteed & direct loans | 0 | 4,201 | 3,756 | 11,771 | 13,354 | 15,553 | 29,274 | 33,277 | 33,664 |
| (Unsubsidized loan share of guaranteed & direct loans) | (0) | (0) | (0) | (0) | (0) | (0) | (11,250) | (14,031) | (14,523) |
| Subtotal | 606 | 6,706 | 9,510 | 19,708 | 21,578 | 2,4215 | 37,693 | 42,357 | 43,605 |
| *Specially directed aid* | | | | | | | | | |
| Social Security | 0 | 2,065 | 3,240 | 3,574 | 0 | 0 | 0 | 0 | 0 |
| Veterans | 357 | 4,639 | 12,391 | 3,253 | 1,305 | 834 | 1,386 | 1,369 | 1,481 |
| Military | 222 | 267 | 287 | 381 | 517 | 453 | 466 | 470 | 484 |
| Other grants | 46 | 66 | 187 | 231 | 102 | 144 | 245 | 265 | 290 |
| Other loans | 0 | 173 | 133 | 118 | 563 | 423 | 346 | 213 | 110 |
| Subtotal | 626 | 7,210 | 16,238 | 7,557 | 2,487 | 1,854 | 2,442 | 2,317 | 2,365 |
| Total federal aid | 1,232 | 13,916 | 25,748 | 27,265 | 24,065 | 26,069 | 40,136 | 44,674 | 45,970 |
| **Other Aid Programs** | | | | | | | | | |
| State grant programs | 299 | 977 | 1,453 | 1,520 | 1,980 | 2,283 | 3,192 | 3,374 | 3,528 |
| Institutional & other grants | 1,437 | 3,463 | 3,464 | 3,083 | 4,475 | 7,073 | 10,041 | 11,389 | 12,209 |
| Non-federal loans | 0 | 0 | 0 | 0 | 0 | 0 | 1,313 | 1,956 | 2,417 |
| Total federal, state, and institutional aid | 2,967 | 18,356 | 30,665 | 31,868 | 30,520 | 35,425 | 54,681 | 61,392 | 64,124 |

*Note:* 1998–1999 data are preliminary.

*Source:* College Board. (1999), p. 7, Table 2, & p. 19, Table B.

billion in 1980 to $12.2 billion in 1998. In contrast, state grants over the same period have increased only about half as much, from $1.5 billion in 1980 to $3.5 billion in 1998. The burgeoning of institutional aid reflects the growing importance of tuition discounting, as schools have used financial aid packages to make their admissions offers to high-achieving students more competitive and financially enticing.

Two important developments in higher education financing emerged in the late 1990s. In response to the easing of fiscal constraints, both the federal government and a number of states began once again to expand their investments in public colleges and universities. These investments were not, however, a simple reversal of the retrenchment of the previous decade. The federal government has poured most of its newly added resources into new federal tax credits for higher education, which are heavily targeted to middle- and upper-middle-income families (see The View from Washington, later in this chapter, and Chapter 3). States, which during the earlier period of stringency cut back on direct appropriations to institutions and on means-tested aid programs, have shown little interest in expanding investments in need-based student aid. Instead, they are focusing new spending on tuition reductions and on programs that, like Georgia's HOPE Scholarships, avoid means testing. Thus, between 1995 and 1998, the real increase in state government spending on need-based aid was 13.2 percent; the real increase in state non-need aid, in contrast, was 58.6 percent (Schmidt, 1997, p. A33; Schmidt, 2000, p. A39).[3]

## Tuition Costs and Financing

In addition to unequal shares of federal, state, and institutional aid available to them, students of varying income levels face significant differentials in tuition costs. The National Postsecondary Student Aid Surveys (NPSAS), conducted for the National Center for Education Statistics, provides detailed student-level data on higher education financing, correlated to family income level and type of school attended (U.S. Department of Education, National Center for Educational Statistics, various years).

*Private Nonprofit Universities*   As Table 5.3 shows, gross tuition charges (sticker prices) at private nonprofit colleges and universities increased considerably in real dollars for students from all income backgrounds over the nine-year period from 1986 to 1995, with the largest absolute increase for upper-income students. However, increases in the net tuition actually paid by students were somewhat smaller than indicated by the sticker prices: $3,482 versus $4,379 for upper-income students; $2,205 versus $3,820 for middle-income students; and $2,084 versus $3,117 for lower-income students.

Federal grants fell in real value for all three income groups, although these grants contributed only a small percentage of gross tuition for students from middle- and upper-income backgrounds. For students from lower-income backgrounds, the decline in the real value of federal grants, along with the real increase in gross tuition, resulted in a considerable decrease in the share of tuition covered by federal grant aid over time—from 22 percent in 1986 to only 14 percent in 1995.

The subsidy value of federal loans (computed at 50 percent of the total loan amount; see McPherson & Schapiro, 1991a) grew for all students attending private nonprofit institutions over this period, reflecting the enormous increase in loans discussed earlier. State grants not only contributed a decreasing share of gross tuition but also declined significantly in real

Table 5.3.
Financing Undergraduate Tuition, 1986–1987 and 1995–1996
(in 1992–93 dollars)

| | | Net Tuition | Federal Grant | Fed. Loan Subsidy | State Grant | Institution al Grant | Gross Tuition |
|---|---|---|---|---|---|---|---|
| **Private Non-profit Institutions** | | | | | | | |
| Lower income | 1986–1987 | $1,446 | $1,658 | $999 | $1,469 | $2,133 | $7,704 |
| | 1995–1996 | 3,530 | 1,525 | 1,308 | 984 | 3,473 | 10,821 |
| Middle income | 1986–1987 | 4,118 | 374 | 879 | 625 | 2,151 | 8,147 |
| | 1995–1996 | 6,323 | 136 | 1,176 | 503 | 3,830 | 11,967 |
| Upper income | 1986–1987 | 7,616 | 130 | 334 | 93 | 977 | 9,151 |
| | 1995–1996 | 1,1098 | 13 | 593 | 88 | 1,738 | 13,530 |
| **Public Institutions** | | | | | | | |
| Lower income | 1986–1987 | (512) | 1,074 | 403 | 415 | 277 | 1,658 |
| | 1995–1996 | (143) | 1,087 | 691 | 505 | 539 | 2,679 |
| Middle income | 1986–1987 | 1,076 | 107 | 310 | 116 | 259 | 1,868 |
| | 1995–1996 | 1,731 | 71 | 569 | 156 | 332 | 2,859 |
| Upper income | 1986–1987 | 1,864 | 36 | 83 | 19 | 138 | 2,140 |
| | 1995–1996 | 3,155 | 3 | 307 | 56 | 209 | 3,730 |
| **Private For-profit (Proprietary) Institutions** | | | | | | | |
| Lower income | 1986–1987 | 1,950 | 1,674 | 1,311 | 330 | 202 | 5,468 |
| | 1995–1996 | 3,539 | 1,414 | 1,328 | 291 | 131 | 6,702 |
| Middle income | 1986–1987 | 4,008 | 168 | 1,363 | 246 | 214 | 6,000 |
| | 1995–1996 | 5,193 | 122 | 1,445 | 141 | 125 | 7,026 |
| Upper income | 1986–1987 | 5,495 | 51 | 408 | 10 | 121 | 6,085 |
| | 1995–1996 | 6,408 | 0 | 729 | 0 | 69 | 7,206 |

*Notes:* (a) Numbers are averages across all full-time dependent students attending a particular institutional type.

(b) Federal loan subsidies are computed at 50% of loan amounts (excluding Parent Loans for Undergraduate Students [PLUS]).

(c) Income brackets: 1986–87: <$23,500; $23,500–$54,900; >$54,900. 1995–96: <$32,600; $32,600–$76,200; >$76,200.

*Source:* Calculated from 1986–87 and 1995–96 National Postsecondary Student Aid Survey databases (U.S. Department of Education, National Center for Education Statistics, various years).

terms (the real value of state grants fell by $485, or 33 percent, for lower-income students). Institutional grants, in contrast, have increased rapidly for students from all income backgrounds, with the largest absolute increase going to middle-income students. The contribution of institutional grants to gross tuition has increased from 28 percent to 32 percent for lower-income students; from 26 percent to 32 percent for middle-income students, and from 11 percent to 13 percent for upper-income students.

*Public Colleges and Universities*    Federal grants for lower-income students attending public colleges and universities were roughly stable, but the percentage of gross tuition covered by federal grant aid fell from 65 percent in 1986 to 41 percent in 1995. The subsidy value of federal loans, in contrast, increased in real terms for students from all income backgrounds, as did the real value of state grants.[4] Although institutional grants are less important in dollar terms at public than at private institutions, they nevertheless increased for students from all income groups.

*Private For-Profit Institutions*    Sticker prices for tuition also increased for students attending private for-profit (proprietary) institutions. However, in this case increases in the net tuition price actually paid by students were about equal to, or were larger than, increases in sticker prices for each income group—$913 versus $1,121 for upper-income students; $1,185 versus $1,026 for middle-income students; and $1,589 versus $1,234 for lower-income students. This reflects the decline in the real value of financial aid from various sources.

*The Role of Student Loans*    The student financing patterns reflected in the 1995 data were largely the result of changes in federal student aid programs introduced in the 1992 reauthorization of the Higher Education Act—the most striking of which is the spectacular run-up in federal loan volume since 1992. As shown in Table 5.2, federal lending has grown in real dollars at a staggering rate during the 1990s, largely because of the creation of the unsubsidized (or "no-need") loan program that permits all enrolled students to borrow to meet educational costs without regard to income or need. In 1998–1999, the unsubsidized program accounted for $14.5 billion, or 43 percent, of the total $33.6 billion in loan volume.

In addition, a set of changes in needs analysis methodology introduced in the 1992 reauthorization of the Higher Education Act increased borrowing in the subsidized, or need-based, loan program. The new rules discount a family's home equity as an asset, with the result that many more students from middle- and upper-middle-income families can qualify as "needy" and receive this aid. Other factors contributing to the ballooning loan program include the rising costs at public institutions and the simplified procedures for obtaining a direct loan.

## Implications for Lower-Income Students

This recent pattern of declining real funding for federal grants, coupled with rapid expansion in subsidized loans, seems to reflect not a deliberate policy shift but, rather, the working out of budgetary pressures. Since grant funds are a form of discretionary spending, their real decline is a result of the general squeeze on the federal budget. Guaranteed loans, by contrast, are an entitlement and so over the short run are not affected in the same way by budget battles.

Intended or not, this shift has significant implications for the targeting of federal aid subsidies. Pell Grants are very effectively targeted to students from lower-income families, as the data show. Federal loan subsidies, in contrast, are distributed much more broadly to students from middle-income as well as lower-income families, with some loan subsidies even going to students from higher-income families. Clearly, the emphasis on loans as a source of higher education funding over the last decade shifts support away from students from lower-income families toward middle- and upper-income Americans.

This trend helps explain why recent increases in enrollment rates have not been uniform across income groups. In a series of important studies, Thomas Kane (1995 & 1998) has documented the differential impact of tuition increases on families of varying economic circumstances through analysis of state, national, and individual data. Kane (1995) notes that the gap in enrollment rates between students from the lowest-income quartile and those from the other three quartiles grew by 12 percent between 1980 and 1993 (p. 6). Additionally, the gap between the enrollment rates of whites and those of African Americans and Hispanics has likewise grown over that period, a fact consistent with the lower average socioeconomic status of these minorities. These findings correlate with the results of our own econometric analysis showing that price sensitivity to enrollment is concentrated among students from lower-income families, with little or no impact on students from higher-income families (McPherson & Schapiro, 1991b).

Net tuition increases of approximately $650 to $1,300 (as shown in Table 5.3) have not deterred students from middle- and upper-income families from enrolling in public institutions, the largest segment of higher education. Economists have long criticized the large subsidies to middle- and upper-income families implicit in the states' tendency to subsidize the cost of college attendance through universally low tuition rates. This evidence is consistent with the judgment that, at the margin, shifting some of the financing burden from state governments to middle- and upper-income families does not discourage enrollment.

The shift of individual student aid from grants to loans over the last decade has probably benefited largely students from middle- and upper-middle-income families at public colleges and universities, mostly in the form of unsubsidized loans. Although these students no doubt welcome such support, there is little evidence that it is essential to their attending college. Yet federal grants targeted to students from lower-income families do influence college enrollment in this group. Therefore, the recent redistribution of federal dollars appears to be going in the wrong direction, both from the standpoint of social equity and of efficiency in promoting college enrollment.

## Stratification of Higher Education

The impact of these trends is made clearer in Table 5.4, which depicts the relationship between the income background of students and the selectivity of the colleges or universities they attend. In 1981, only 10.0 percent of all first-time full-time students from lower-income families and 13.7 percent from lower-middle-income families were enrolled as freshmen at medium or highly selective four-year institutions. Comparable figures for students from upper-income and highest-income families were 36.9 percent and 44.4 percent, respectively. By 1999, the proportion of students from the lower-income groups that were enrolled at medium or highly selective schools rose to 15.5 percent and 16.7 percent, whereas percentages for their affluent counterparts reached 39.1 percent and 51.1 percent. Thus, at most one in six students from lower-or lower-middle-income families is currently enrolled at a medium or highly selective four-year institution, in contrast to over one out of two from the wealthiest families.

Furthermore, although all institutions of higher learning subsidize the education of students to some extent, the more elite the school, the greater the gap between student fees and the actual cost of the education. The degree of subsidy can be understood as a proxy for the value of the education in terms of future income and less tangible "life chances" of graduates. Gordon Winston and his colleagues (Winston, Carbone, & Lewis, 1998) found that in 1995 the average higher education institution spent $12,209 (educational and general expenditures plus a capital use cost) while charging a tuition sticker price of $6,135. That implies that all students, regardless of whether they received financial aid, were awarded a general subsidy of $6,074. The average financial aid award was $2,251, producing an average total subsidy of $8,324, the difference between educational costs of $12,209 and net tuition of $3,885.

Subsidies vary much more within sectors than across them. The average subsidy at a private institution is only modestly higher than one in the public sector ($8,653 versus $8,029). The more selective a university, how-

## Table 5.4
## Distribution of Freshman Enrollment by Income Category and Institutional Selectivity, 1981 and 1999

| 1981 | Lower <$10.1K | Lower Middle $10.1K–$15.2K | Middle $15.2K–$30.3K | Upper Middle $30.3K–$50.5K | Upper $50.5K–$101.1K | Richest >$101.1K | All Groups |
|---|---|---|---|---|---|---|---|
| 2-year public | 44.6% | 41.4% | 39.3% | 31.2% | 20.4% | 13.2% | 35.6% |
| 2-year private | 6.2 | 5.5 | 4.2 | 3.6 | 3.5 | 3.0 | 4.3 |
| Low-Select 4-year | 39.3 | 39.3 | 38.0 | 38.7 | 39.1 | 39.4 | 38.6 |
| Medium-Select 4-year | 7.0 | 10.1 | 13.7 | 18.4 | 22.1 | 23.9 | 14.8 |
| High-Select 4-year | 3.0 | 3.6 | 4.9 | 8.1 | 14.8 | 20.5 | 6.7 |
| | 100.0 | 100.0 | 100.0 | 100.0 | 100.0 | 100.0 | 100.0 |
| **1999** | <$20K | $20K–$30K | $30K–$60K | $60K–$100K | $100K–$200K | >$200K | |
| 2-year public | 39.0% | 38.8% | 35.5% | 29.8% | 16.8% | 10.1% | 30.9% |
| 2-year private | 3.7 | 2.7 | 2.4 | 1.8 | 2.2 | 3.5 | 2.4 |
| Low-Select 4-year | 41.9 | 41.8 | 41.8 | 42.4 | 42.0 | 35.4 | 41.7 |
| Medium-Select 4-year | 9.7 | 11.5 | 14.9 | 18.0 | 23.1 | 25.6 | 16.5 |
| High-Select 4-year | 5.8 | 5.2 | 5.4 | 8.0 | 16.0 | 25.5 | 8.5 |
| | 100.0 | 100.0 | 100.0 | 100.0 | 100.0 | 100.0 | 100.0 |

*Notes:* (a) The survey of freshmen in 1999 reflected family income in the 1998 calendar year, whereas the survey of freshmen in 1981 reflected family income in the 1980 calendar year. Inflation between 1980 and 1998 equaled 97.9%.

(b) The selectivity definitions vary somewhat across institutional categories. We define low selectivity as having the following SAT ranges: <1050 for private universities; <1025 for private nonsectarian 4-yr. colleges; <1050 for Protestant 4-yr. colleges; <1025 for Catholic 4-yr. colleges; <1000 for public universities; and <1025 for public 4-yr. colleges. We define medium selectivity as having the following SAT ranges: 1050–1174 for private universities; 1025–1174 for private nonsectarian 4-yr. colleges; >1049 for Protestant 4-yr. colleges; >1024 for Catholic 4-yr. Colleges; 1000–1099 for public universities; and >1024 for public 4-yr. colleges. We define high selectivity as having the following SAT ranges: >1174 for private universities; >1174 for private nonsectarian 4-yr. colleges; and >1099 for public universities.

*Source:* Calculated from results of the American Freshman Survey (Cooperative Institutional Research Program, various years).

ever, the greater its subsidy. Two-year public institutions provide an average subsidy of $7,371; private comprehensives offer an average subsidy of $5,862. Liberal arts colleges subsidize students by an average of $9,622. Both public and private research universities, which are the most selective, provide subsidies of well over $10,000 per student. When analyzed by degree of subsidy, it is apparent that students from affluent families are far more likely to attend the more selective—and highly subsidized—four-year research institutions than are students from lower-income families.

## A CHANGING NATIONAL IDEOLOGY

The recent trends in higher education financing, enrollment rates, and attendance patterns are the visible manifestations of shifting social and political assumptions regarding our shared national commitment to equity in educational access, as well as the best methods for achieving this goal within the context of competing national priorities. Recent developments, such as the movement of the federal government into the realm of tuition tax credits and the emergence of financial aid wars among Ivy League universities, highlight this changing consciousness, but the transformation itself is broader and deeper than these headline-making events.

## Underlying Assumptions

Since the 1960s, Americans have espoused the goal of college financing as that of meeting need. Scholarships for needy and deserving students have been part of higher education for many decades, but the idea that the higher education system should systematically and objectively measure need for financial assistance and then find the means to meet that need is a distinctly modern one.

Following World War II and the Korean War, the GI Bill introduced Americans to the concept that the opportunity to attend college should not be limited by the student's income or social status. The flood of veterans into the colleges and universities also led to substantial expansion of capacity in the late 1940s and early 1950s. When enrollments tapered off in the mid-1950s, a number of prestigious institutions found their campuses competing for attractive students. Impelled by a desire to stem the loss of dollars on the one hand and a commitment to broadened opportunities in the wake of the GI Bill experience on the other, a number of eastern universities collaborated to find a systematic means of measuring what each family could contribute toward college expenses. The result of these efforts was the formation of the College Scholarship Service, an entity that grew out of the College Board, to develop criteria for measuring need as objectively as possible. The gap between the family contribution and the annual cost of attendance at a particular school was the student's "need," and the finance system was envisioned as filling the gap.

A number of premises underlie this worldview. It is supposed, first, that financial considerations should be attenuated, if not eliminated, when families decide whether and where their children should attend college. From this perspective, an ideally operating financial aid system would do away with cost as a factor in college decisions, both by eliminating differences across schools for a given needy family and by bringing the price within reach for that family. A second assumption is that the family's ability to pay is being measured at the point when a student reaches college age—

that is, with late adolescents in mind as students and with parents as the financially responsible parties. Third, this perspective invites us to see "unmet need" as a shared responsibility—a challenge governments, colleges, and donors should work together to meet.

This ideology has been of great importance in shaping the American understanding of higher education in recent decades. There are, to be sure, important aspects of American higher education that fit uneasily into this framework. For example, the influential principle of low tuition for public higher education derives from a quite different starting point: That affordability should be achieved through keeping prices low for all, rather than tailoring the price to ability to pay. Additionally, the financing of part-time education for adults is hard to reconcile with this approach, as the messy and jury-rigged modifications of needs analysis for these students make clear. Few schools in any era have possessed the combination of resources and conviction to fully realize the principles embedded in the commitment to "meet full need."

All that being said, the influence of this conceptual framework remains impressive. The role of the College Board in helping to advance this set of goals, both among colleges and in Washington, has been key. Thus, when the federal government in 1965 began to explore means to help students pay for college on a continuing basis, rather than piecemeal as a way of recognizing veterans, "unmet need" played a critical role, first in determining eligibility for subsidized loans and then in allocating grant funds. States also participated, as they developed need-based grant programs of their own. The picture of a student getting through college with the help of a package of need-based aid assembled from federal, state, and institutional resources is very familiar, and it reinforces the concept of a partnership among sectors to bolster equal access.

In concert with the overall excellence of our college and university system, this assumption has helped to make U.S. higher education unique in the world. Some countries, including Sweden, do not believe that parents should be responsible for the cost of their children's higher education. Those countries that have systematically subsidized higher education based on ability to pay, like Australia and now (to some extent) England, tend to finance school prospectively through a graduate tax or income-contingent loan framework. This approach, of course, shifts the burden to the students themselves during a later part of their lives, when their earning power is presumably enhanced.

It is also clear that many of the policy disputes of the last several decades have really been "family quarrels" within an overall framework of agreement on the needs principle. Thus, public and private institutions have argued over how stringent needs analysis should be. Private institutions, who can handcraft exceptions for their smaller numbers of cases, and who are largely handing out their own money, have tended to be parsimonious in providing aid. Mass-production public institutions that are largely passing through government money have been more generous. Even major policy disagreements, like those over the Middle Income Student Assistance Act in the late 1970s and the Reagan-era budget struggles, were largely fought out over how to interpret and apply conceptions of need.

## Shifting Institutional Priorities

This fundamental assumption—that opportunity should accompany ability and desire for higher education, in whatever socioeconomic strata they are found—is changing now, in ways that are hard to mistake. Over the last ten to fifteen years colleges and universities (and the consulting industry that supports and is supported by them) have responded to intensified competition for students by adopting an instrumental view of aid as part of an enrollment management strategy. Rather than seeking to eliminate price as a factor in college choice, which is the official ideology in "meeting need," schools are turning the net price to their advantage in the competitive struggle (McPherson & Schapiro, 1997).

Of particular interest has been the growth of merit aid, especially if that term is considered broadly. In the narrow sense, merit aid is typically understood as the granting of a scholarship to an individual student strictly because of his or her aptitude—intellectual, musical, athletic, and so on—without regard to financial need. In practice, however, need-based awards increasingly include a merit component. Many schools, for example, will adjust the financial aid package offered to a needy student based on his or her attractiveness. Less capable students may receive an aid award that falls short of measured need, or a package that meets need only with a very large loan component.

Even more seriously, institutions are increasingly making the determination that a student is eligible for any need at all depending on that student's desirability, using less stringent criteria for more attractive students. This practice subverts the goal of providing an objective and scientific measurement of need and tends to undermine the need ideology itself. The U.S. Congress has encouraged this trend by manipulating federal definitions of need for grant and loan programs, at least in part to appease politically influential groups. The clearest example is dropping home equity out of the federal needs analysis; in following suit, institutions offer a break to particularly desirable students by using the federal methodology in determining need.

Such practices at prestigious leaders in American higher education—Princeton, Harvard, Yale, Stanford, and MIT, for example—have attracted public attention. In the last few years, each of these institutions has announced policies and practices that depart in significant ways from standard needs analyses developed in the profession. These range from changing the treatment of home equity, to modifying the handling of retirement assets, to promising to negotiate with families who get better aid offers elsewhere.

The universities that have introduced these policies are quick—and correct—to assert that they are doing so not to harm their competitors but to respond to their own needs and those of the families they aim to serve. Of course, this is exactly the point: The whole idea of an *agreed* system of needs analysis is to limit the ability of individual schools to pursue their own interests, so that they may better serve the common interest. When each school defines for itself what the measurement of need will be, the idea of an objective measurement of need, as well as the idea of a coordinated system, is called into doubt.

Until fairly recently, leading private universities had a means of securing agreement among themselves about how to interpret need: the "overlap meetings," where the treatment of individual cases was compared. When the U.S. Department of Justice ended this arrangement in the early 1990s with an antitrust lawsuit, the department's aim presumably was to produce the result we now see: universities pursuing their individual self-interest, instead of acting collectively. In fact, the competitive maneuverings of Harvard, Yale, and others are exactly what an economist would predict when cooperative arrangements are suspended. Unfortunately, it is far from clear that a benevolent invisible hand is assuring that this is an arena where the pursuit of individual self-interest serves the collective good. In any event, the Ivy League schools are latecomers to the use of financial aid as a competitive strategy. The rest of the industry is well ahead in using merit aid, preferential and differential packaging, idiosyncratic measurement of need, and other techniques to make their aid dollars serve institutional self-interest.

## The View from Washington

The drift of individual colleges and universities away from the underlying premises of need-based student aid parallels the changes in the structure of government aid programs. As we have seen, state governments, which have in the past put limited dollars into need-based aid, have increasingly diverted these resources to other ends. A number of states created programs modeled after Georgia's HOPE Scholarship, which substitutes merit for need as the basis for awarding grants, and which funds all students whose high school performance exceeds certain thresholds provided they stay in state to go to college (see Chapter 4). Even more attractive politically are programs of college savings or prepaid tuition, which target those who can afford to save for college and provides them with access to federal tax benefits.

These state-sanctioned federal tax subsidies pale in comparison to the federal tax credits introduced in the 1998 tax year by the Taxpayer Relief Act of 1997. The new tax benefits, focused on middle- and upper-middle-income families that have substantial tax liabilities to be offset, instantly became the largest federal program supporting higher education—larger than outlays on Pell Grants and larger than the federal cost of subsidized loans. The same legislation also expanded several federal tax subsidies for college savings and introduced tax deductions for college loan repayments.

The most important part of this law is the creation of the Hope Scholarship tax credit, which allows families to deduct 100 percent of tuition expenses, less any grant aid, up to $1,000, and 50 percent of any remaining tuition expenses up to $2,000, from the taxes they are required to pay. The credit is for tuition only—room and board are excluded—and it applies only to the first two years of college. The program phases out for families with incomes between $80,000 and $100,000 and for single filers with incomes between $40,000 and $50,000. In addition, the Lifelong Learning Tax Credit program allows qualified taxpayers to deduct from the taxes they owe 20 percent of the tuition they pay for any form of postsecondary education beyond the first two years of college, up to a maximum of $5,000 (scheduled to rise to $10,000 in 2003). Income limits are the same as for the Hope Scholarship.

Both of these tax credits are nonrefundable—that is, the credit is available only to the extent that a family has a net tax payment to offset. (Refundable credits like the Earned Income Tax Credit include net payments to families whose tax payments fall short of the amount of credit for which they are eligible.) This rule sharply reduces the value of the credit to lower-income families whose tax liability does not rise to the level of the educational tax credits. Another provision lowers the available Hope Scholarship tax credit by a dollar for every dollar of grant received, further reducing eligibility for lower-income students. The largest benefits from both credits will accrue to families with incomes from $60,000 to $80,000 whose members attend expensive private colleges and universities.

The introduction of these credits represents a sharp shift in the direction of federal policy. On two previous occasions, in the mid-1960s and the late 1970s, the U.S. Congress gave serious consideration to tax credits for college tuition. In each case, Congress decided in favor of modifying the system of student aid expenditures instead of resorting to the tax system.

From a policy perspective, using the tax system to subsidize the college costs of middle- and upper-middle-income students is highly inefficient. Empirical evidence shows, as noted above, that lower-income students are more sensitive to the price of college attendance than are students from more affluent backgrounds. A large fraction of the tax dollars expended on these credits will benefit families who would have made the same educational choices without the credit. Moreover, the credits are likely to induce public community colleges to raise their tuition to $2,000 in order to qualify their students fully for the Hope Scholarship credit; likewise, the Lifelong Learning Credit may encourage institutions to offer various forms of recreational programming to adults, with 20 percent of the cost borne by the U.S. government. Virtually all public policy analysts agree that rational goals for promoting investment in higher education could be better achieved through expanded grant programs than through these tax credits.

## Politics and Policy

Why, then, did the tax credits succeed? The decision in 1997 to turn to the tax system instead of greatly expanding funding for the Pell Grant program is difficult to understand on public policy grounds, but it is easier to make sense of in political and institutional terms. Institutionally, the U.S. Congress biases spending decisions in favor of tax expenditures over direct expenditures. The so-called balanced budget rules require identifying a specific offset to any increase in spending in any discretionary government program, but they do not similarly require offsets for tax expenditures. From a pragmatic point of view, large increases in spending on student aid grants would have been nearly impossible to achieve, whereas building consensus for tax credits was relatively straightforward. (Congress did increase the maximum value of Pell Grants by $300 at the same time it passed the tax credits, with a net effect of adding $10 to tax spending for every dollar added to Pell Grants.)

Politically, the Democratic administration proposed the tax credits to appeal to middle-income voters as an alternative to reductions in the capital gains tax that was favored by Republicans. From the standpoint of higher education lobbying groups, the issue was presented not as tax credits versus increases in grants but as tax breaks for higher education consumers versus tax breaks for others. Framed in this way, several of the major higher education lobbying groups in Washington were eager to support the credits.

The increase in economic returns associated with higher education over the past two decades no doubt also contributed to the political popularity of the tax credits. These high returns motivate families to invest in further education, even in the face of rising prices. The large numbers of middle- and upper-middle-income families with members in college increase the political payoff to easing the financial burden of those investments. During the late 1980s and early 1990s, public institutions, which enroll almost 80 percent of American college students, raised prices as state legislative funding fell. It is perhaps ironic that the effect of the new federal tax credits is largely to substitute federal expenditures for these reductions in state spending on higher education—a peculiar example of reverse federalism.

The decision by Congress and former president Bill Clinton to open the federal tax code to higher education subsidies may prove fateful. In the U.S. system, direct expenditures are subject to relatively close annual scrutiny, whereas tax expenditures are much more loosely overseen. Under current arrangements, tax credits are heavily targeted toward relatively affluent families, who are more likely to vote and are more politically influential than the lower-income families who are the major clients of Pell Grants. Given these political realities, Congress may over time expand the tax credits program and be increasingly less forthcoming in funding Pell Grants. Such continued redirection of education resources away from the neediest students would weaken both access to, and choice of, higher education alternatives for lower-income families. At the same time, since aid affects college attendance for middle- and upper-income families only marginally, such a development would ease the financing burden on affluent Americans without increasing the national investment in higher education.

In sum, the federal government, state governments, and colleges and universities themselves have backed away from the commitment to measure and meet financial need that has dominated thinking about higher education finance in this country since the 1960s. Structural shifts in the targeting of aid have played an important role, we believe, in the declining access to and increasing stratification in higher education discussed earlier. Acceleration of these trends in the years ahead would result in growing inequalities of income and opportunity in our nation.

## THE FUTURE OF INSTITUTIONALLY BASED AID

The allocation of institutionally based financial aid is only one factor, and not the dominant one, in shaping the distribution of college opportunity.

Still, it is clear that a variety of forces have converged to reduce the emphasis of institutional aid on meeting students' need and to increase the proportion of that aid devoted to middle- and upper-income students. As Table 5.3 shows, students from middle-income families at private institutions received the largest increase in institutional aid between 1986 and 1995, with an average boost of almost $1,700.[5] The increase for lower-income students was less than $1,300, and even upper-income students received an average increase of over $750.

In a previous study we examined the use of explicitly non-need awards, a type of aid that is heavily used by universities in search of competitive advantage (McPherson & Schapiro, 1998). We found rapid growth in non-need aid in both public and private sectors over the period from 1983 to 1991. A clear pattern emerges from the data: The more selective institutions (in 1983) had the highest growth rates of non-need aid. Those public institutions that described entrance as "very difficult" raised their spending per freshman on non-need grants by 20 percent per year after adjusting for inflation, whereas those rated "minimally difficult" raised their spending by only 9 percent annually. Nonetheless, it was still true in 1991–1992 that the largest number of dollars spent per freshman on non-need aid was at the least selective among the public institutions ($311), an amount that was two-and-a-half times the level of spending at the most selective public schools ($124).

In private higher education, the most selective institutions reported virtually no spending on non-need awards. The least selective institutions had the highest spending on non-need awards in 1983, but increased their spending on non-need aid by only 1 percent annually to 1991, whereas other categories of institutions raised their spending quite rapidly. In 1983, the least selective schools spent $500 to $600 more per enrolled freshmen on non-need aid than did other private institutions; by 1991, that gap had shrunk to $250 or so, with schools that are "moderately difficult" to enter actually spending more per student than the least prestigious institutions.

Although we have not had an opportunity to update these data, recent work by Donald E. Heller (2001) suggests that non-need aid continues to be an important factor in student finance. Heller finds that in the 1989–1995 period non-need aid grew more slowly in total dollars than need-based aid. However, he identifies a trend toward fewer and larger non-need grants, which he attributes to greater use of non-need or merit awards as an explicit competitive strategy. The very rapid growth in spending on non-need aid in general, and academic merit aid specifically (except at the most selective private colleges and universities), is perhaps the most significant finding here. These data indicate that non-need aid is becoming a more important competitive factor for a wide range of institutions.

It is easy to understand why the most selective and prestigious institutions invest less in merit aid than do other institutions. These institutions face a substantial excess demand for admission, rejecting two, three, or more applicants for every one they accept. Given that many of these rejected applicants would be paying the full tuition price if admitted, the opportunity cost of merit awards is quite high: Rather than the alternative to a merit student being an empty bed, the alternative is a student who brings respectable credentials and a substantial tuition payment.

As we have emphasized, non-need aid is only a partial indicator of the extent to which colleges use aid as a competitive device. Other enrollment management strategies are less easy to measure quantitatively. However, many indicators suggest that colleges are departing further and further from the kind of aid award practices that a simple focus on meeting need would imply.

These trends are no doubt dismaying to many college leaders, and especially to student aid officials, most of who feel strong professional and ethical commitments to a need-based aid system. It is important to understand, however, that most universities and colleges have very little ability to influence this situation by their individual actions. The market for college students is highly competitive. Putting aside the handful of colleges with extraordinarily large endowments, most private colleges are highly dependent on tuition revenues to cover their costs. If a single institution were to depart sharply from its competitors' practices, say, by cutting back on aid offers to more affluent students and expanding its aid to high-need students, it would quickly lose enrollment and tuition revenue. The resulting decline in resources would have a further negative effect on the ability to attract students and would tend to force the school into a downward spiral. Individual colleges are in this respect much more creatures of their environment than they are masters of their own fate.

## A Way Back?

The obvious response to such a dilemma is collective action, an agreement to act on common principles in awarding aid. Just such a search for collective agreement is, of course, what underlay the original formal needs analysis systems developed in the 1950s. It is clear that the antitrust prosecution of the Overlap Group in the early 1990s has made schools much more wary of entering into formal agreements to conform their student aid policies to common standards. Even without such legal concerns, however, competitive pressures would make it difficult for colleges to find their way back to more principled allocation of aid according to need.

One reason is that colleges have become much more sophisticated in applying techniques to gain maximum competitive advantage from student aid. These tools make much clearer to colleges what the opportunity cost of more rule-bound policies would be. At the same time, presidents and chief financial officers have come to take a stronger interest in financial aid policies than they did in an earlier era, increasing the pressure to search for competitive advantage. A further consideration is that the market for colleges is more fluid and more national than it was forty years ago. Few schools can now rely on any captive market, whether of local students or of co-religionists, and this has increased competitive energies.

In light of the legal, economic, and sociological forces inclining schools toward student aid competition, any realistic strategy for moving schools toward a renewed commitment to common standards of needs assessment and award practices would require two components. First, the legal uncertainties surrounding such cooperation would need to be clarified. Even in current law, a narrowly constructed provision assures institutions that are completely need-blind in admission of U.S. freshmen that they can agree on standards of need measurement without fear of antitrust prosecution. A substantial expansion of this provision would encourage greater cooperation among colleges.

Second, a successful strategy would also need to address the growing economic incentives toward merit competition and competitively determined needs assessment. Elsewhere, we have sketched a mechanism that the federal government could use for this purpose (McPherson & Schapiro, 1997). The essential idea is to create a supplemental federal grants program targeting students attending schools that adhere to need-based principles in awarding institutional aid. This second step involves some technical complexities, but those are far from insurmountable. The presence of such an award program would improve the alignment between the individual interest of colleges in advancing their own economic welfare, and the broader social goal of targeting aid to needy students. Such an initiative would help restore the sense that the federal government and colleges are partners in striving to meet students' needs for financial assistance.

A program along these lines could garner widespread support from college ,and universities; it would also be a more efficient and equitable use of federal funds than, for example, the current educational tax credits. Such a program would be an important step toward realizing the goals and values of our need-based student aid ideology. It is, however, a real question whether the nation possesses the political and social will to pursue this course.

## Reexamining Our Premises

A realistic answer to the question just posed may be no. Thirty years is a long time for a particular conceptual framework to hold sway in a changing political environment. If restoration of a commitment to the principles of need-based aid is unreachable, it may well be time to question key assumptions underlying the need-based aid system. One of these is that parents have an important responsibility to help finance their children's education; another is that an assessment of ability to pay should look backward to parents' resources, rather than forward to students' future earnings. Even more importantly, it may be necessary to challenge the most fundamental tenet underlying our system of higher education finance: that family financial circumstances should not be a principal determinant of children's educational opportunities.

These are principles that have, on balance, served our nation well in the last thirty years. They are, however, very unevenly applied in American higher education at this time. It is always dangerous when avowed principles become seriously out of line with observed practices. In American higher education finance, these are dangerous times.

## NOTES

1. This analysis draws upon and updates our book, *The Student Aid Game* (McPherson & Schapiro, 1998).

2. All years shown refer to the fall of each academic year; that is 1979 is academic year 1979–1980.

3. For more information on this subject, see Chapter 4.

4. Note that for the average lower-income student attending a public institution the contribution of federal, state, and institutional aid exceeded the gross tuition price in both years, once the subsidy value of federal loans is included as part of financial aid. This reflects the difference between gross tuition and gross total costs of attendance, with the latter including room, board, and other charges. Thus, the excess of financial aid over gross tuition is applied against other costs of attendance.

5. Recall that these are averages across students, both those who do receive aid and those who do not.

## REFERENCES

College Board. (1998). *Trends in student aid: 1998*. Washington, DC: Author.
College Board. (1999). *Trends in student aid: 1999*. Washington, DC: Author.

Cooperative Institutional Research Program. (Various years). *American freshman survey*. Los Angeles: University of California, Los Angeles.

Heller, D. E. (2001). Race, gender, and institutional financial aid awards. *Journal of Student Financial Aid, 31*(1), 7–24.

Kane, T. J. (1995, July). *Rising public college tuition and college entry: How well do public subsidies promote access to college?* Working Paper No. 5164. Cambridge, MA: National Bureau of Economic Research.

Kane, T. J. (1998). Taking stock at the end of three decades of federal financial aid. Unpublished manuscript. Cambridge, MA: Harvard University, Kennedy School of Government.

McPherson, M. S., & Schapiro, M. O. (1991a). *Keeping college affordable: Government and educational opportunity*. Washington, DC: Brookings Institution.

McPherson, M. S., & Schapiro, M. O. (1991b). Does student aid affect college enrollment? New evidence on a persistent controversy. *American Economic Review, 8*(1), 309-18.

McPherson, M. S., & Schapiro, M. O. (1997). Financing undergraduate education: Designing national policies. *National Tax Journal, 50*(3), 557–71.

McPherson, M. S., & Schapiro, M. O. (1998). *The student aid game: Meeting need and rewarding talent in American higher education*. Princeton, NJ: Princeton University Press.

Schmidt, P. (1997, April 11). States' student-aid spending slackened in 1995–96, survey says. *Chronicle of Higher Education*, A33.

Schmidt, P. (2000, April 21). Boom in merit-based scholarships drives 8.8% rise in state funds for student aid. *Chronicle of Higher Education*, A39.

U.S. Department of Education, National Center for Education Statistics. (1999). *Digest of Education Statistics, 1998*. Washington, DC: Author.

U.S. Department of Education, National Center for Education Statistics. (Various years). *National postsecondary student aid survey*. Washington, DC: Author.

Winston, Gordon C., Carbone, Jared C., & Lewis, Ethan G. (1998, March). *What's been happening to higher education? Facts, trends, and data: 1986–87 to 1994–95*. Paper DP-47. Williamstown, MA: Williams Project on the Economics of Higher Education Discussion.

# PART III

## Early Intervention, Remediation, and Support Services

# CHAPTER

# Pre-college Outreach and Early Intervention Programs

*Laura W. Perna and Watson Scott Swail*

A ccess to higher education has increased dramatically over the past three decades. More than 12 million undergraduates were enrolled in colleges and universities nationwide in 1998, nearly twice as many as in 1969 (National Center for Education Statistics, 2001). Growth has occurred at both two-year and four-year colleges and universities and among students of all income groups. The number of low-income individuals attending the nation's college and university students is higher today than ever before.

Despite some progress, however, lower-income students continue to be less likely than higher-income students to enroll in and graduate from college. Although college enrollment rates increased by 15 percent between 1980 and 1999 for 18- to 24-year-old high school graduates in the lowest family income quartile, college enrollment rates continue to be substantially lower for students from the lowest family income quartile than for students in the highest family income quartile (57 percent versus 86 percent in 1999, Mortenson 2001). The current 30 percent gap in college enrollment rates between low- and high-income students is comparable to the size of the gap in the 1960s (Gladieux & Swail, 1999; see Chapter 1 for more on the gap in college participation rates).

The income gap is even larger in degree attainment than in enrollment. Using data from the Census Bureau and the High School and Beyond longitudinal survey of 1980 high school sophomores, Mortenson (2001) estimated that only 22 percent of individuals from the lowest family income quartile who had enrolled in college would earn a bachelor's degree by age

24, compared with 78 percent of individuals from the highest family income quartile. Data from the Beginning Postsecondary Student Survey show that 41 percent of first-time full-time freshmen in 1989 with high socioeconomic status attained a bachelor's degree within five years, compared with only 6 percent of first-time full-time freshmen with low socioeconomic status (Berkner, Cuccaro-Alamin, & McCormick, 1996).

Gaps in college enrollment and degree completion rates by family income have persisted despite more than three decades of effort by the federal government to eliminate the gaps. Federal intervention at the postsecondary level has historically focused on reducing economic barriers to higher education to ensure that no academically qualified citizen is denied access to college because of limited financial resources. The centerpiece of the federal government's effort is Title IV of the Higher Education Act of 1965, which provides financial assistance in the form of grants, loans, and work-study to students attending postsecondary educational institutions in the United States. The federal government's commitment to student aid is demonstrated by the magnitude of the resources devoted to these programs. Two-thirds of federal on-budget outlays for postsecondary education in fiscal year (FY) 1996 were for student financial assistance and Federal Family Education Loans (Hoffman, 1997), and two-thirds of the $68 billion in federal, state, and institutional aid awarded to students in 1999–2000 was subsidized by the federal government (College Board, 2000).

The persistence of gaps across income groups in college enrollment and degree completion despite the dedication of large amounts of federal resources suggests that the traditional focus on financial barriers has been too narrow. Although insufficient financial resources clearly play a role, increasing college access and success also requires attention to the steps required to be academically, socially, and psychologically prepared to enter and succeed in college (Gladieux & Swail, 1999). Early intervention programs offer this type of comprehensive approach.

This chapter reviews the importance of a more comprehensive approach to college access, provides examples of existing programs, and discusses the effectiveness of these programs. Although more research is needed to identify the most effective aspects of early intervention programs, a review of what is known about the facilitators and barriers to college enrollment strongly suggests that only a comprehensive approach to increasing college access and degree completion such as that offered by early intervention programs will effectively ensure equal educational opportunity for all individuals regardless of family income.

## IMPORTANCE OF INCREASING COLLEGE ACCESS AND DEGREE COMPLETION RATES

Both individuals and society at large benefit from college enrollment and degree completion. Individuals who attend and graduate from college realize economic and non-economic benefits in both the short- and long-term. The short-term consumption benefits of attending college include enjoyment of the learning experience, involvement in extracurricular activities, participation in social and cultural events, and enhancement of social status. Long-term or future benefits include higher lifetime earnings, more fulfilling work environment, better health, longer life, more informed purchases, and lower probability of unemployment (Bowen, 1997; Leslie & Brinkman, 1988; McPherson, 1993). Fully realizing the economic returns to higher education requires not only enrolling in college but also persisting to degree completion (Adelman, 1999; Pascarella & Terenzini, 1991).

Sustained public support for early intervention programs is justified not only because of the economic and non-economic benefits that accrue to individuals but also because of the societal benefits that result from increased levels of educational attainment. Although societal benefits are more difficult to quantify than are individual benefits, benefits that "spillover" beyond the individual cannot be ignored (Bowen, 1997). Society benefits from the economic growth that results from the enhanced productivity of labor associated with higher levels of educational attainment. Another type of societal benefit is neighborhood effects. Such benefits include reduced crime, reduced dependency on public welfare and Medicaid, increased volunteerism, higher voting rates, and greater civic involvement. Based on his comprehensive assessment of the public and private benefits of higher education, Bowen (1997) concluded that the single most important effect of higher education is intergenerational, an effect that is manifested most clearly in terms of the increased educational attainment of one's children.

## PREDICTORS OF COLLEGE ENROLLMENT

The reliance of the federal government upon student financial aid as the primary means for increasing college access assumes that economic variables are the most important determinants of college enrollment. Economic approaches posit that an individual makes a decision about attending college by comparing the benefits with the costs for all possible alternatives and then selecting the alternative with the greatest net benefit, given the individual's personal tastes and preferences (Manski & Wise, 1983; Hossler, Braxton, & Coopersmith, 1989; Paulsen, 1990).

Clearly, family income and financial resources influence college enrollment decisions. Researchers have consistently found that students with lower levels of socioeconomic status, a composite measure that reflects students' family income as well as their parents' level of educational attainment and occupational status, are less likely than other students to plan to pursue postsecondary education and actually enroll in college (Cabrera & La Nasa, 2001; Hossler, Braxton, & Coopersmith, 1989; Kane, 1994; Kane & Spizman, 1994; Manski & Wise, 1983; Rouse, 1994). Students from lower-income families have also been found to be less likely than other students to realize their educational plans by enrolling in higher education and persisting to degree attainment (Hossler, Schmit, & Vesper, 1999; Perna, 2000b).

Nonetheless, a review of enrollment trends and prior research suggests that merely making financial aid available to low-income students is not enough to ensure that all students have equal access to the benefits associated with earning a college degree (Gladieux & Swail, 1999). Researchers have found that in addition to financial resources, college enrollment decisions are influenced by educational expectations, academic achievement and preparation, parental support and encouragement, and knowledge and information about college and financial aid (Cabrera & La Nasa, 2001; Perna, 2000b). Through the use of status attainment models, sociologists have shown that educational aspirations are among the most important predictors of college enrollment (Boyle, 1965; Sewell, Haller, & Ohlendorf, 1970; Alwin & Otto, 1977; Falsey & Heyns, 1984; Sewell, Hauser, & Wolf, 1986).

Both economists and sociologists have found academic achievement to be an important predictor of college enrollment (Becker, 1962; Sewell, Haller, & Ohlendorf, 1970; Alexander & Eckland, 1974; Catsiapis, 1987; Hossler, Braxton, & Coopersmith, 1989; St. John & Noell, 1989; St. John, 1991; Kane & Spizman, 1994; Rouse, 1994; Perna, 2000a). Economic approaches to college enrollment predict that low levels of academic achievement during the pre-college years reduce the likelihood that a student will successfully complete the educational program and obtain a job producing the expected future earnings premium, whereas sociological status attainment models posit that academic achievement is related to the amount of encouragement for higher education that a student receives from teachers, counselors, and parents.

Differences in academic preparation are also an important source of observed differences in college enrollment and persistence rates. Adelman (1999) concluded that the quality and intensity of the high school curriculum is a more important predictor of bachelor's degree completion than test scores or class rank. Using an index of academic qualifications representing cumulative grade point average in academic courses, senior class rank, aptitude test scores, and SAT or ACT test scores, Berkner and Chavez (1997) showed that a substantially smaller share of students from low-income families than of students from high-income families (53 percent versus 86 percent) were qualified to attend a four-year college or university.

Lack of knowledge and information about college, a manifestation of social capital, has also been shown to be an important predictor of college enrollment. Most studies show that parents and students overestimate college costs and lack accurate information about financial aid (McColloch, 1990; Litten, 1991; Ikenberry & Hartle, 1998). After controlling for other variables related to college enrollment decisions, some research shows that students are less likely to enroll in college when their parents lack accurate knowledge and information about financial aid (Ekstrom, 1981; Higgins, 1984; Flint, 1993). Parents with lower incomes and lower levels of education have been shown to be less knowledgeable about various types of financial aid even after controlling for differences in such variables as language spoken at home, parents' educational expectations for the child, and whether another child was currently attending college (Olson & Rosenfeld, 1984). Cabrera and La Nasa (2000) concluded based on their review and synthesis of prior research that lower-income students generally rely on fewer sources of information about college and are less knowledgeable about college costs and financial aid than their higher-income peers.

## DEFINING EARLY INTERVENTION PROGRAMS

More comprehensive than traditional student financial aid programs, early intervention programs are designed to provide low-income and other disadvantaged groups of students with the opportunity to develop the skills, knowledge, confidence, aspirations, and overall preparedness for college early enough in their schooling so as to influence their ultimate educational attainment levels. Such programs are sponsored by the federal government, state governments, not-for-profit organizations, and individual colleges and universities (Fenske et al., 1997; Perna, Fenske, & Swail, 2000).

### Federally Sponsored Programs

The federal government has played a critical role in developing pre-college outreach and early intervention programs. Established as part of the original "War on Poverty" during the Johnson administration, the federal TRIO programs are designed to help disadvantaged students prepare for and enter higher education. As mandated by Congress, two-thirds of the students served by TRIO programs must come from families with incomes below $24,000. Authorized by Congress in 1964 as part of the Educational Opportunity Act, Upward Bound provides students with academic instruction on college campuses after school, on Saturdays, and during the summer. In 1995–1996, 601 Upward Bound programs served 44,700 students (U.S. Department of Education, 2001a).

Established during the authorization of the Higher Education Act in 1965, Talent Search and the Student Support Services programs were added to Upward Bound to form the core of the TRIO programs. Talent Search, which served nearly 300,000 sixth- through twelfth-grade students at 319 sites across the nation in FY1996 (U.S. Department of Education, 2001a), provides participants and their families with information regarding college admissions requirements, scholarships, and financial aid. In 1995–1996 705 Student Support Services projects provided counseling and remedial training to 165,300 students attending college (U.S. Department of Education, 2001a). President Bush requested a 7 percent increase for the TRIO programs for FY2002, an increase intended to raise total appropriations for the TRIO programs from $730 million for FY2001 to $780 million for FY2002 (U.S. Department of Education, 2001b).

In 1992 the federal government expanded its commitment to early intervention programs by authorizing the National Early Intervention Scholarship Program (NEISP). The NEISP offered matching grants to states for programs providing financial incentives, academic support services and counseling, and college-related information to disadvantaged students and their parents. Programs were funded under the NEISP in California, Indiana, Maryland, Minnesota, New Mexico, Rhode Island, Vermont, Washington, and Wisconsin. At least six other state governments have sponsored early intervention programs beyond those funded through NEISP (Fenske, Geranios, Keller, & Moore, 1997).

As part of the 1998 reauthorization of the Higher Education Act, Congress established a new program, Gaining Early Awareness and Readiness for Undergraduate Programs (GEAR-UP), to supercede the NEISP. Unlike the NEISP, which awards grants only to states, GEAR-UP grants are also available to partnerships comprised of (1) one or more local educational agencies representing at least one elementary and one secondary school; (2) one institution of higher education; and (3) at least two community organizations, which may include businesses, philanthropic organizations, or other community-based entities. The GEAR-UP legislation also includes the 21st Century Scholars Certificate program. This program, originating from a bill written by Congressman Chaka Fattah (D-PA) and later endorsed and retitled by President Clinton as the High Hopes program, notifies low-income sixth- to twelfth-grade students of their expected eligibility for federal financial assistance under the Pell Grant program. In FY1999 $120 million was appropriated for GEAR-UP, a substantial increase over the $3.6 million provided for NEISP in FY1998. Over 670 partnerships applied for the first GEAR-UP grants in 1999, and 180 awards were made. Congress appropriated $200 million for FY2000 and $295 million for FY2001. Nonetheless, President Bush requested only $227 million for GEAR-UP for FY2002, 23 percent less than the amount appropriated for FY2001 (U.S. Department of Education, 2001b).

## Non-government Programs

Early intervention programs are also sponsored by non-governmental entities, including private organizations, foundations, and colleges and universities. One of the most prominent private early intervention programs is Eugene Lang's I Have a Dream (IHAD) program, established in 1981. The program originated when Lang, visiting his former East Harlem elementary school, spontaneously guaranteed the sixty-one students in his presence the financial support to attend college if they graduated from high school. Today 175 projects in sixty-two cities in twenty-six states across the nation serve more than 13,000 students from low-income communities by providing such services as tutoring, mentoring, academic enrichment, cultural and recreational activities, and individual attention from as early as the second grade through high school graduation, as well as partial financial assistance for college (I Have a Dream Foundation, 2001). The IHAD program has not only supported the students participating in particular programs but also led other philanthropists and agencies to establish similar programs.

Colleges and universities also play an important role in early intervention. A 1994 survey by the U.S. Department of Education revealed that about one-third of all colleges and universities offer at least one program designed to increase access for educationally or economically disadvantaged pre-collegiate students (Chaney, Lewis, & Farris, 1995). A 1999 survey sponsored by the College Board suggests that one-fourth of the programs targeting low-income students receive financial support from colleges and universities, and more than one-half of the programs receive in-kind support from colleges and universities (Perna, 2002).

Table 6.1
Percentage of Early Intervention Programs That Target Low-income Students Who Receive Various Sources of Financial and In-kind Support

| Source | Financial support | In-kind support |
|---|---|---|
| Federal government | 56.8 | 1.8 |
| AmeriCorps | 3.1 | 4.7 |
| State government | 25.8 | 11.6 |
| Local government | 6.6 | 8.0 |
| Local school system | 10.4 | 37.9 |
| Community organization | 8.7 | 19.1 |
| Business/industry | 17.1 | 16.9 |
| Private foundations | 21.4 | 6.6 |
| Individuals | 15.3 | 13.8 |
| Colleges/universities | 26.1 | 56.4 |
| Fundraising | 14.9 | 6.6 |
| Other | 5.4 | 4.9 |

*Source*: Swail and Perna (2000).

## EFFECTIVENESS OF EARLY INTERVENTION PROGRAMS

Among the challenges associated with early intervention programs that have been identified by program administrators are sustaining funding, hiring and retaining effective staffs, and incorporating current technology (Swail & Perna, 2000). Sustaining financial support is obviously critical to the continued viability of early intervention programs. Data from the College Board's 1999 survey suggest that external sources are the primary source of funding for 72 percent of the early intervention programs targeted at low-income students. Less than 2 percent rely primarily on tuition and fees for financial support. Table 6.1 shows that the most common sources of financial support are the federal government, state governments, colleges and universities, and private foundations. The most common sources of in-kind support are colleges and universities and local school systems.

Program administrators also indicate that program staffing is critical to the success of their programs (Swail & Perna, 2000). Among the related issues are hiring personnel who support the mission and goals of the organization and providing ongoing professional development. The College Board survey indicates that about 80 percent of the programs serving low-income students have five or fewer full-time paid staff (Perna, in press). Although focus groups with program administrators suggest that many programs have high staff turnover rates (Swail & Perna, 2000), the College Board survey showed that only 13 percent of programs that target low-income students believed training or recruiting program staff was a somewhat or high problem area (Perna, 2002).

The knowledge and use of computers and other information technologies is an emerging issue for many programs. Programs need to build strategic plans for purchasing, upgrading, and effectively utilizing technology. Although most outreach programs focus on developing academic skills, program administrators believe that more attention should be given to developing the technological capacity that complements knowledge acquisition (Swail & Perna, 2000).

Although nearly all (95 percent) programs targeting low-income students report that they conduct program evaluations (Perna, 2002), these evaluations are typically no more than a tally of the numbers of students participating in particular activities. One exception is a six-year longitudinal study of Upward Bound conducted by Mathematica Policy Research (Myers & Schrim, 1999). This study showed that program participants generally had higher educational attainment expectations, earned more credits in mathematics and social studies during high school, earned more non-remedial credits from four-year colleges, earned fewer remedial credits from two-year colleges, and were more involved with various college activities. The study also suggested that the benefits were greater for participants from low-income families, as well as for participants who had lower initial educational expectations and lower levels of academic achievement. Nonetheless, the study also revealed important challenges. For example, participation appeared to have no impact on high school grade point average, high school graduation, or college enrollment. Moreover, about 37 percent of participants dropped out during the first year of an Upward Bound program and fewer than 45 percent of participants were expected to continue in the program through their senior year of high school (Myers & Schirm, 1999).

In contrast to the Upward Bound evaluation, other evaluations have found that college enrollment rates are higher for program participants than for non-participants (Fenske et al., 1997). Using data from the National Educational Longitudinal Study (NELS), Horn (1997) showed that participating in any type of outreach program during high school nearly doubled the odds of enrolling in a four-year college or university among at-risk 1992 high school graduates after controlling for other college preparation activities, parental involvement, student involvement, and peer association.

Differences in assessments of the effectiveness of early intervention programs may be attributable, at least in part, to the great variety across programs in terms of the services offered. Services offered by early intervention programs include college awareness; social skills development; career counseling and exploration; preparatory, supplemental, accelerated, and/or college-level courses; life skills and goal setting; information about college and financial aid; campus visits and tours; cultural activities; information for parents; tutoring and remediation; critical thinking skills; and admissions test training (Chaney et al., 1995; Swail & Perna, 2000). Some programs also include some type or amount of financial benefit, such as full or partial tuition scholarships, book grants, and other financial aid. This variation in the components of individual programs complicates the task of determining which aspects are most important to the overall effectiveness of a program.

Cabrera and La Nasa (2001) speculated that the most effective intervention strategies are likely to be comprehensive in terms of the scope of services offered and holistic in terms of the school-based and family-based resources that are utilized. Nonetheless, only a fraction of pre-college outreach programs appear to address what the literature shows are the most important predictors of college enrollment. Perna (2002) found that only 25 percent of programs targeting low-income students have five critical components: (1) the goal of college attendance (to facilitate educational expectations); (2) college tours, visits, or fairs (to facilitate knowledge and information about college); (3) the goal of promoting rigorous course-taking (to facilitate academic preparation and achievement); (4) a parental involvement goal (to facilitate parental support and encouragement); and (5) early outreach, beginning by the eighth grade (to facilitate curricular planning). In order to ensure that scarce resources are being used as efficiently and effectively as possible, further research is required to determine the combination of incentives, support services, and program components that is most effective in increasing access to and completion of college for low-income students.

Early intervention programs also differ in terms of the grade level at which students initially become involved. Whereas program administrators (Swail & Perna, 2000) and some researchers (e.g., Levine & Nidiffer, 1996) assert that early intervention programs must start early, more research is required to determine the most appropriate level at which students should initially become involved in an early intervention program. According to the College Board's survey, the most common entering grade for programs that target low-income students is the ninth grade (Perna, 2002). About 9 percent begin in elementary school grades, 33 percent in middle school, 28 percent in ninth grade, and 29 percent in later high school grades. Cabrera and La Nasa (2000) concluded, based on their review and synthesis of prior research, that the college choice process begins as early as the seventh grade and that the process of becoming academically qualified for college begins as early as the eighth grade. Because available resources are limited, research should examine the incremental benefits and costs associated with beginning programs at various grade levels.

Programs also differ in terms of the characteristics of students targeted for participation, particularly whether student eligibility criteria are limited to financial need and other related risk factors or whether students should also exhibit some level of academic ability. Based on their evaluation of Maryland's pilot College Preparation Intervention program, the Institute for Higher Education Policy (1994) recommended that student eligibility be defined in terms of both academic and economic criteria. Suggested academic criteria include standardized test scores, grade point average, and recommendations from teachers and counselors. This report concluded that by selecting only students with college potential, this program would differentiate itself from other programs that target all disadvantaged students, such as Upward Bound. Nationwide more than one-third (38 percent) of programs targeting low-income students also specifically target only those students with middle or high academic achievement (Perna, 2002). Only 7 percent of programs targeting low-income students also specifically target students with low academic achievement.

The level of parental involvement also varies across early intervention programs. Program administrators (Swail & Perna, 2000) generally believe that parents play a critical role in the success of their programs. Among programs that target low-income students, three-fourths offer a parental component and one-fourth require parental participation (Perna, 2002), likely reflecting research showing that parental support and encouragement for higher education are important predictors of college enrollment (Hossler, Braxton, & Coopersmith, 1989; Hossler, Schmit, & Vesper, 1999), particularly among students at risk of dropping out of high school (Choy et al., 2000). Despite the general consensus about the value of involving parents, programs vary in terms of the particular services offered to parents, with 63 percent offering "college awareness," 56 percent offering participation in student activities, and 52 percent offering financial aid counseling (Perna, 2002). Based on their examination of one university-sponsored program, Tierney and Jun (2001) concluded that by actively involving parents as well as by incorporating other aspects of their cultural backgrounds, college preparation programs may increase their likelihood of success by affirming students' identities. Further research is required to understand not only the particular ways in which parents influence program outcomes but also the ways in which administrators can effectively encourage parents to become involved.

Finally, programs vary in the degree to which they leverage existing re-sources and services to maximize program benefits. One-fifth of programs that target low-income students report that coordinating with partnering agencies is a somewhat or high problem area or area of need (Perna, 2002). Collaboration is limited by the wide range of program sponsors and the small size of most programs. One study found that the median number of students served by the largest program administered by an individual col-lege or university was eighty-two (Chaney et al., 1998).

## CONCLUSION

Some may argue that early intervention programs are too expensive, serve too few students, and are too inefficient, given the high program dropout rates found in the Upward Bound evaluation conducted by Mathematica Policy Research (Myers & Schrim, 1999). Clearly, more needs to be learned about how to structure the most effective early intervention program, par-ticularly with regard to the services offered, grade level to begin services, characteristics of targeted students, how to involve parents, and how to in-crease coordination with other organizations. Nonetheless, because many of these programs appear to have at least some of the components that the literature suggests promote college access and degree attainment, early in-tervention programs offer a ray of hope for those who are interested in iden-tifying policies and practices that effectively increase access to and com-pletion of college for low-income students and other groups that have been traditionally underrepresented in higher education. Although the impor-tance of addressing students' financial needs must not be minimized, focus-ing only on the financial barriers to college access and success is insufficient. A review of trends in college enrollment and degree completion rates shows that interventions that rely exclusively on making financial assistance avail-able to students to attend college have not provided equal opportunity for individuals with low family incomes to access the individual-level economic and non-economic benefits associated with earning a college degree.

One of the most important issues pertaining to early intervention pro-grams is ensuring that adequate financial support is sustained. Although Pres-ident Bush's FY2002 budget requested continued support for the TRIO pro-grams, the proposed 23 percent reduction in federal support for GEAR-UP is troubling. The fact that only 5 percent of the 11 million Americans eligi-ble for services through the TRIO programs are being served because of fed-eral funding limitations (Council for Opportunity in Education, 1996) sug-gests that more, not fewer, resources should be allocated to early intervention programs.

Although more research is required to identify the particular attributes and characteristics of the most effective early intervention programs, support for and commitment to these comprehensive programs must be sustained. By continuing to support early intervention programs while engaging in rigorous systematic research on a range of different programs, we will be working to ensure that the costs of these programs are more than offset by the resulting short- and long-term benefits that are realized not only by individual participants, but also by society at large.

# REFERENCES

Adelman, C. (1999). *Answers in the tool box: Academic intensity, attendance patterns, and bachelor's degree attainment.* Washington, DC: Office of Educational Research and Improvement, U.S. Department of Education.

Alexander, K. L., & Eckland, B. K. (1974). Sex differences in the educational attainment process. *American Sociological Review, 30*(October), 668–82.

Alwin, W. F., & Otto, L. B. (1977). High school context effects on aspirations. *Sociology of Education, 50, 259–73.*

Becker, G. S. (1962). Investment in human capital: A theoretical analysis. *Journal of Political Economy, 70* Supplement(5), 9–49.

Berkner, L. K., & Chavez, L. (1997). *Access to postsecondary education for the 1992 high school graduates.* NCES 98-105. Washington, DC: U.S. Department of Education, National Center for Education Statistics.

Berkner, L. K., Cuccaro-Alamin, S., & McCormick, A. C. (1996). *Descriptive summary of 1989–90 beginning postsecondary students: 5 years later.* NCES 96-155. Washington, DC: U.S. Department of Education, National Center for Education Statistics.

Bowen, H. (1997). *Investment in learning: The individual and social value of American higher education.* Baltimore, MD: Johns Hopkins University Press.

Boyle, R. P. (1965). The effect of the high school on students' aspirations. *American Journal of Sociology, 71, 628–39.*

Cabrera, A. F., & La Nasa, S. M. (2000). Understanding the college-choice process. In A. F. Cabrera and S. M. La Nasa (eds.), *Understanding the college choice of disadvantaged students* (pp. 5–22). San Francisco, CA: Jossey-Bass Publishers.

Cabrera, A. F., & La Nasa, S. M. (2001). On the path to college: Three critical tasks facing America's disadvantaged. *Research in Higher Education, 42*(2), 119–49.

Catsiapis, G. (1987). A model of educational investment decisions. *Review of Economics and Statistics, 69, 33–41.*

Chaney, B., Lewis, L., & Farris, E. (1995). *Programs at higher education institutions for disadvantaged students.* NCES 96-230. Washington, DC: U.S. Department of Education, Office of Educational Research and Improvement.

Choy, S. P., Horn, L. J., Nuñez, A. M., & Chen, X. (2000). Transition to college: What helps at-risk students and students whose parents did not attend college. In A. F. Cabrera, & S. M. La Nasa (eds.), *Understanding the college choice of disadvantaged students* (pp. 31–44). San Francisco, CA: Jossey-Bass Publishers.

College Board. (2000). *Trends in student aid, 2000.* New York: Author.

The Council for Opportunity in Education. "About TRIO." Web page, 1996 [accessed March 2001]. Available at www.trioprograms.org/home.html.

Ekstrom, R. (1981, March). Attitudes toward borrowing and participation in post-secondary education. Paper presented at the Association for the Study of Higher Education Annual Meeting, Washington, DC.

Falsey, B., & Heyns, B. (1984). The college channel: Private and public schools reconsidered. *Sociology of Education, 57*(April), 111–22.

Fenske, R. H., Geranios, C. A., Keller, J. E., & Moore, D. E. (1997). *Early intervention programs: Opening the door to higher education.* ASHE-ERIC Higher Education Report, Vol. 25, No. 6. Washington, DC: George Washington University, Graduate School of Education and Human Development.

Flint, T. (1993). Early awareness of college financial aid: Does it expand choice? *Review of Higher Education, 16*(3), 309–27.

Gladieux, L., & Swail, W. S. (1999). Financial aid is not enough: Improving the odds for minority and low-income students. In J. E. King (ed.), *Financing a college education: How it works, how it's changing* (pp. 177–97). Phoenix, AZ: Oryx Press.

Higgins, A. S. (1984). Who knows and who goes: Student knowledge of federal financial aid programs and college attendance. *Journal of Student Financial Aid, 14*(3), 19–26.

Hoffman, C. M. (1997). *Federal support for education: Fiscal years 1980 to 1996.* NCES 97-384. Washington, DC: U.S. Department of Education, National Center for Education Statistics.

Horn, L. J. (1997, October). *Confronting the odds: Students at risk and the pipeline to higher education,* NCES 98-094. Washington, DC: U.S. Department of Education, National Center for Education Statistics.

Hossler, D., Braxton, J., & Coopersmith, G. (1989). Understanding student college choice. In John Smart (ed.), *Higher education: Handbook of theory and research, Vol. V* (pp. 231–88). New York: Agathon Press.

Hossler, D., Schmit, J., & Vesper, N. (1999). *Going to college: How social, economic, and educational factors influence the decisions students make.* Baltimore, MD: Johns Hopkins University Press.

I Have a Dream Foundation (2001). I Have a Dream Foundation homepage. (http://www.ihad.org).

Ikenberry, S., & Hartle, T. (1998). *Too little knowledge is a dangerous thing: What the public thinks and knows about paying for college.* Washington, DC: American Council on Education.

Institute for Higher Education Policy. (1994). *Evaluation of the College Preparation Intervention Program: A report to the Maryland Higher Education Commission*. Washington, DC: Author.

Kane, T.J. (1994). College entry by blacks since 1970: The role of college costs, family background, and the returns to education. *Journal of Political Economy, 102*(5), 878–911.

Kane, T., & Spizman, L.M. (1994). Race, financial aid awards, and college attendance: Parents and geography matter. *American Journal of Economics and Sociology, 53*(1), 73–97.

Leslie, L.L., & Brinkman, P.T. (1988). *The economic value of higher education*. New York: American Council on Education, MacMillan Publishing Company.

Levine, A., & Nidiffer, J. (1996). *Beating the odds: How the poor get to college*. San Francisco, CA: Jossey-Bass Publishers.

Litten, L.H. (1991). *Ivy bound: High-ability students and college choice*. New York: College Board.

Manski, C., & Wise, D.A. (1983). *College choice in America*. Cambridge, MA: Harvard University Press.

McColloch, S.K. (1990). The financial planning gap. *Journal of College Admissions, 127*, 12–17.

McPherson, M.A. (1993). How can we tell if financial aid is working? In M.O. Shapiro, G.C. Winston, & M.S. McPherson (eds.), *Paying the piper: Productivity, incentives, and financing in U.S. higher education*. Ann Arbor: University of Michigan Press.

Mortenson, T. (2001, April). Trends in college participation by family income: 1970 to 1999. *Postsecondary Education OPPORTUNITY*, pp. 1–8.

Myers, D., & Schrim, A. (1999). *The impacts of Upward Bound: Final report for Phase I of the national evaluation*. Washington, DC: U.S. Department of Education, Planning and Evaluation Services.

National Center for Education Statistics. (2001). *Digest of education statistics: 2000*. NCES 2001-034. Washington, DC: U.S. Department of Education.

Olson, L., & Rosenfeld, R.A. (1984). Parents and the process of gaining access to student financial aid. *Journal of Higher Education, 55*(4), 455–80.

Pascarella, E.T., & Terenzini, P.T. (1991). How college affects students: Findings and insights from twenty years of research. San Francisco, CA: Jossey-Bass Publishers.

Paulsen, M. (1990). *College choice: Understanding student enrollment behavior*. ASHE-ERIC Higher Education Report No. 6. Washington, DC: George Washington University, School of Education and Human Development.

Perna, L.W. (2002). Pre-college outreach programs: Characteristics of programs serving historically underrepresented groups of students. *Journal of College Student Development, 43*(1), 64–83.

Perna, L.W. (2000a). Differences in the decision to attend college among African Americans, Hispanics, and Whites. *Journal of Higher Education, 71*(2), 117–41.

Perna, L. W. (2000b, April). Racial/ethnic group differences in the realization of educational plans. Paper presented at the annual conference of the American Educational Research Association, New Orleans, LA.

Perna, L. W., Fenske, R. H., & Swail, W. S. (2000). Sponsors of early intervention programs. *The ERIC Review: Early intervention: Expanding access to higher education*, 8(1), 15–18.

Rouse, C. E. (1994). What to do after high school: The two-year versus four-year college enrollment decision. In R. G. Ehrenberg (ed.), *Choices and consequences: Contemporary policy issues in education* (pp. 59–88). Ithaca, NY: IRL Press.

Sewell, W. H., Haller, A. O., & Ohlendorf, G. W. (1970). The educational and early occupational status attainment process: Replication and revision. *American Sociological Review*, 35, 1014–27.

Sewell, W. H., Hauser, R. M., & Wolf, W. C. (1986). Sex, schooling and occupational status. *American Journal of Sociology*, 86(3), 551–83.

St. John, E. P. (1991). What really influences minority attendance? Sequential analysis of the High School and Beyond sophomore cohort. *Research in Higher Education*, 32(2), 141–58.

St. John, E. P., & Noell, J. (1989). The effects of student financial aid on access to higher education: An analysis of progress with special consideration of minority enrollments. *Research in Higher Education*, 30(6), 563–81.

Swail, W. S., & Perna, L. W. (2000). A view of the landscape: Results of the national survey of outreach programs. In *Outreach program handbook 2001*. New York: College Board.

Tierney, W. G., & Jun, A. (2001). A university helps prepare low income youths for college: Tracking school success. *Journal of Higher Education*, 72(2), 205–25.

U.S. Department of Education (2001a). *Biennial report: 1995–96*. (http://www.ed.gov/Biennial/95–96).

U.S. Department of Education (2001b). *Department of Education fiscal year 2002 president's budget*. (http://www.ed.gov/offices/OUS/Budget02/Summary/HigherED.html).

# CHAPTER 7

# Beyond Money:
# Support Strategies for
# Disadvantaged Students

*David W. Breneman and Jamie P. Merisotis*

I ncreasing the participation of lower-income and minority students in education beyond the high school level has been an important public policy goal since the passage of the Higher Education Act of 1965. In the past three decades, much apparent progress has been made. The proportion of students enrolling in postsecondary institutions immediately after high school grew from nearly 50 percent in 1972 to 65 percent in the late 1990s. Specifically, lower-income and minority students made gains. In 1996, 49 percent of lower-income students enrolled in college immediately after graduating from high school, up from 26 percent in 1972; black and Hispanic student enrollment rose from 45 percent for each group to 56 percent and 51 percent, respectively (U.S. Department of Education, 2000).

Although these numbers are encouraging, they mask two important caveats. First, despite significant increases in college enrollments for lower-income and minority students in recent years, the gaps in college enrollment between the lowest and highest incomes and between whites and those of other races have not changed measurably in the last twenty-five years. Second, although more lower-income and minority students are enrolling in colleges and universities, many may not be able to complete their degrees. For example, in 1998 only 18 percent of black and 17 percent of Hispanic high school graduates age 25 to 29 had a bachelor's degree, compared to 35 percent of their white counterparts (U.S. Department of Education, 2000).

Public policy at the state and federal levels, as well as institution-based strategies, has focused on a combination of remediation and support, in addition to financial aid programs, to improve the chances of these students to attain a college degree. For example, many institutions offer developmental coursework and other services to assist students who come to college underprepared in specific subject areas. Support aids include tutoring and mentoring to help students with the transition into college and throughout their postsecondary education careers.

This chapter summarizes knowledge about these two intervention strategies. Both remediation and support services target nonfinancial factors that block successful transition to college or that may inhibit student success once enrolled. Although remediation and support programs can have an important impact on overall national success in improving access to higher education for underserved populations, such strategies must be aligned with public and institutional policies.

## REMEDIATION

Offering coursework below college level in higher education institutions is coming under increased scrutiny in the public policy environment. Variously referred to as "remedial education," "developmental education," "college prep," or "basic skills," remedial programs have become the subject of much debate, with policymakers asking why so many students in institutions of higher learning are studying basic "reading, writing, and arithmetic"—subjects that should have been learned in high school, if not junior high school. A number of states, including Colorado, California, Florida, Georgia, Louisiana, Massachusetts, New York, Oklahoma, Tennessee, and Virginia, have over the past several years attempted to limit remedial education. In 1998, the trustees of the City University of New York (CUNY) voted to phase out most remedial education in the system's 11 four-year institutions. Since its implementation in September 1999, the CUNY plan has moved ahead steadily.

Following similar patterns, some states such as Florida have moved virtually all remediation to community colleges. Legislators in Texas and other states are expressing concern that tax dollars are being used in colleges to teach high school courses. Legislatures in New Jersey, Montana, Florida, and Oregon, among others, are considering proposals that would require public school systems to pay for any remedial work a public school graduate must take in college.

A survey of state legislators reflects concern about the number of students requiring remedial coursework. Most lawmakers are uncertain, however, about what to do. Asked whether colleges and universities should give remedial education more attention, 34 percent of legislators disagreed, 32 percent agreed, and 32 percent were neutral. Although most state legislators believe that the problem is inherited from the K–12 sector, whom to hold responsible and how are not so obvious (Ruppert, 1996).

This confusion is mirrored by educators. Proponents and opponents alike point to the effect that remedial education has upon the quality, accountability, and efficiency of higher education institutions. The effects of remediation on diversity, educational opportunity, and enrollment are being debated in several venues. Unfortunately, the quality of these discussions is diminished by the lack of agreement on the nature of remediation; little consensus and understanding exist about what remedial education is, whom it serves, who should provide it, and how much it costs. This vagueness often renders public policy discussions ill-informed at best.

Furthermore, recent research reveals that remediation is not so much a problem for ordinary citizens as an issue for elite opinion makers (Mazzeo, 2001). Strong positions are taken both for and against remediation in the debates, suggesting that this topic has considerable ideological significance. The politics of remediation may, therefore, be more important in determining policy than disinterested analysis of costs and benefits. Nonetheless, this chapter frames the discussion to the extent possible in cost-benefit terms, a context we believe is readily applicable to the issues of public investment that are involved.

## DEFINITIONS

College remediation incorporates a wide array of students and activities, and it can include assessment and placement, curriculum design and delivery, support services, and evaluation. The discussion of remedial education often evokes the image of courses in reading, writing, and mathematics whose content is below "college level." But the term "college level" suggests that agreed-upon standards exist, or at least enjoy a consensus, among educators. A reasonable assumption would be that the academic community has identified specific knowledge and skills that are required of students if they are to be successful in a college or university. Conversely, if students do not possess the specified knowledge and skills, they need remedial education in order to attain academic success.

The fact is that remedial education is in the eye of the beholder. Rather than based on some immutable set of college-level standards, remedial education more often than not is determined by the admissions requirements of the particular institution. More precisely, remediation at a community college with open admissions is not the same as remediation at a doctoral research institution. As Astin (1998, p. 13) points out:

> Most remedial students turn out to be simply those who have the lowest scores on some sort of normative measurement—standardized tests, school grades, and the like. But where we draw the line is completely arbitrary: lowest quarter, lowest fifth, lowest 5 percent, or what? Nobody knows. Second, the "norms" that define a "low" score are highly variable from one setting to another.

A case in point is the twenty-one-campus California State University (CSU) system. Although state policy in California requires that students entering CSU be in the top third of their high school graduating class, the *Los Angeles Times* reported that 47 percent of the fall 1997 freshman class required remedial work in English and 54 percent needed remedial work in mathematics (Trombley, Doyle, & Davis, 1998).

Other issues that complicate the discussion include the wide age range of recipients, the large numbers of recent immigrants enrolled, and the degree of the remediation needed. On the first point, much of the discussion implies that the students involved are all recent high school graduates, whose schools (elementary, middle, or high schools) have failed them. The reality, however, is more complex, for nearly 50 percent of all remedial students are over the age of 24 (McCabe, 2000). A 35-year-old adult who takes college classes may need brush-up work in mathematics simply because of years of non-use. Similarly, some newly arrived immigrants will need remedial work, which is no reflection on the quality of U.S. high schools.

Finally, the research clearly calls for distinctions in degrees of remedial needs. Students who need help with reading are most severely deficient, for that skill is basic to virtually all college work. Remedial work for writing and mathematics is rarely as severe a problem for future success in college. Work by Adelman (1999) and McCabe (2000) both point to these differences in subsequent performance, with students who are seriously deficient having far less success than those who primarily need brush-up work.

## HISTORY

Given the increased attention to remedial education, it is easy to conclude that efforts to provide compensatory education to underprepared students in colleges and universities are recent phenomena that somehow reflect the present condition of postsecondary education in the nation. Although some individuals may argue that the quality of the higher education enterprise has decreased over the years, the fact remains that remedial education has been part of higher education since early colonial days.

## Early Patterns

Dating back to the seventeenth century, Harvard College provided tutors in Greek and Latin for those underprepared students who did not want to study for the ministry. Indeed, many of the early colleges were more like academies than institutions of higher learning, providing preparatory work under the college name. The middle of the nineteenth century saw the establishment of land grant colleges, which instituted preparatory programs or departments for students below average in reading, writing, and mathematics (Payne & Lyman, 1998). In 1849, the first remedial education programs were offered at the University of Wisconsin (Breneman & Haarlow, 1998). By the end of the nineteenth century, when only 238,000 students enrolled in all of higher education, more than 40 percent of college freshmen participated in pre-collegiate programs (Ignash, 1997).

Because of increased competition for students among higher education institutions in the beginning of the twentieth century, underprepared students were accepted at growing rates. For instance, over half of the students enrolled in Harvard, Princeton, Yale, and Columbia did not meet entrance requirements and were placed in remedial courses. Later, the need for remedial education surged in the wake of the vast influx of World War II veterans taking advantage of the GI Bill. Also, thousands of underprepared students enrolled in colleges and universities from the 1960s to the 1980s in response to open admissions policies and government funding following the passage of the Civil Rights Act of 1964 and the Higher Education Act of 1965 (Payne & Lyman, 1998).

## Recent Approaches

A comprehensive survey of remediation in higher education conducted by the National Center for Education Statistics (NCES) in 1995 provides evidence of this reality (U.S. Department of Education, 1996). The study defined remedial programs as courses in reading, writing, and mathematics for college students lacking those skills necessary to perform at the level required by the institution. Thus, the constitution of remedial courses varied from institution to institution. The following points detail the study's major findings:

- Over three-quarters (78 percent) of higher education institutions that enrolled freshmen in fall 1995 offered at least one remedial reading, writing, or mathematics course. All public two-year institutions and almost all (94 percent) institutions with high minority enrollments offered remedial courses.

- Twenty-nine percent of first-time freshmen enrolled in at least one remedial reading, writing, or mathematics course in fall 1995. Freshmen were more likely to enroll in a remedial mathematics course than in a remedial reading or writing course, irrespective of institution attended.

- At most institutions, students did not take remedial courses for extended periods of time: two-thirds of the institutions indicated that on average students were enrolled in remedial courses for less than one year; 28 percent indicated that the average time was one year; and 5 percent reported that the average time was more than one year.

- Many students taking remedial courses were still able to qualify for federal financial aid because the courses were registered for institutional credit, although not for degree credit. (U.S. Department of Education, 1996)

Because NCES conducted similar surveys for the academic year 1983–1984 and fall 1995, it is possible to compare the intensity of remedial education course offerings over the past decade. The consistency in the patterns is striking. In 1983–1984, 82 percent of the institutions offered remedial education in all three areas (reading, writing, and mathematics), compared to 78 percent in fall 1995. Sixty-six percent provided remedial reading courses in 1983–1984 compared to 57 percent in fall 1995; for remedial writing, 73 percent and 71 percent; and remedial mathematics, 71 percent and 72 percent, respectively (see Figure 7.1). Statistics for first-time freshmen enrolled in remedial courses were not estimated for the academic year 1983–1984; however, 30 percent of first-time freshmen enrolled in all three remedial courses in fall 1989, compared to 29 percent in fall 1995.

Because remediation has always been with us, it is worth asking why it has become the focus of so much attention and heated debate in recent years. In our view, it was inevitable that the criticism of public schooling that has dominated discussion for the past fifteen to twenty years would move to the college level in the form of attacks on remedial education. This move is simply the logical extension of the criticism leveled at K–12 education. The presence of remediation in college becomes yet another reason for condemning the schools (and the colleges as well).

Clearly, improved K–12 education over time should reduce the need for remediation for recent graduates, but as we have noted earlier, there are

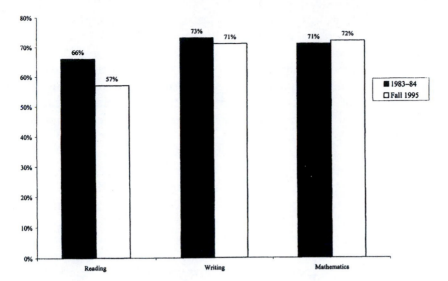

*Figure 7.1 Percent of Institutions Offering Remedial Courses, 1983–1984 Academic Year and Fall 1995*

Source: U.S. Department of Education (1996).

many other adult students for whom the need will remain. We think proper policy debates should focus on which institutions are best equipped to perform remediation and who should pay for it, rather than simply on criticism and denial. Evaluation of the costs and benefits of remedial education within a nonideological framework is most likely to lead to the right policy decisions in this contentious area.

## DEMOGRAPHICS

### Students

As we have noted, a substantial proportion of postsecondary education students are 25 years of age or older, and many of these adult students are enrolled in remedial courses. The exact proportion or number of older students requiring remedial education, however, is difficult to discern, and the data on age distribution of remedial students vary widely from state to state. One national study has found that 46 percent of students enrolled in remedial programs are over the age of 24 (Saxon & Boylan, 2000, as cited in McCabe, 2000).

Data from individual states support the NCES findings. For instance, Maryland found that more than three-fourths of remedial students in the community colleges in 1994–1995 were 20 years of age or older (Maryland Higher Education Commission, 1996). In Florida, it was reported that 80 percent of the students in remedial classes were not recent high school graduates but, rather, older students who needed to brush up their skills, usually in mathematics, before entering the higher education mainstream (Trombley, Doyle, & Davis, 1998).

Figure 7.2 indicates that 60 percent of students enrolled in remedial programs are white, 23 percent are African American, and 12 percent are Hispanic (McCabe, 2000, p. 5). The same study reports that female enrollment slightly exceeds male enrollment, and that 54 percent of remedial students have annual family incomes below $20,000 (McCabe, 2000). There are no surprises here; these are people who need and seek postsecondary education for the skills required to advance in a demanding labor market. The enhancement of human capital and its associated costs are reasonable considerations in evaluating this activity, but one should not lose sight of important values of equity and opportunity, equally central to the American story.

## Institutions

The most recent NCES survey reported that remediation takes place in all community colleges, in four out of five public four-year institutions, and in more than six out of ten private four-year institutions (U.S. Department of Education, 1996). Although most community colleges accept remediation as an essential part of their mission, controversy surrounds its role in four-year institutions. In the highly publicized case of the City University of New York, the aim was to remove remedial courses from the four-year campuses, relegating such work (and the students who need it) to two-year campuses and private for-profit providers. This approach makes some sense on a theoretical level and, if successful students are able to transfer with ease to a four-year college, might be a satisfactory resolution of the issue. Many observers are concerned, however, that transfer patterns are far from perfect, and many who start in two-year colleges never make the shift, thus failing to complete bachelor's degrees. This is a difficult topic on which to generalize because transfer patterns differ dramatically across the country. It seems unlikely that there is a single, best solution to be applied everywhere; instead, each state, locality, and institution needs to consider carefully in setting policy.

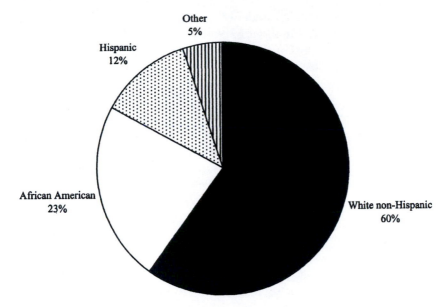

*Figure 7.2 Enrollment in Remedial Education Program by Race*

Source: McCabe (2000).

## COSTS

A recent analysis suggests that remedial education absorbs about $1 billion annually in a public higher education budget of $113 billion—less than 1 percent of expenditures. (Breneman, 1998). This estimate was based on extrapolations from the few states that had reasonable cost data and included the costs associated with remediation for both traditional-age freshmen and returning adult students. Follow-up work that involved contacts with all fifty states produced no evidence that this estimate was far off the mark, although the bias in reported data is almost certainly to underreport costs somewhat (Breneman & Haarlow, 1998).

Among states, the percentage of remedial education expenditures comprising the total budgets for higher education showed wide variance. In fiscal year (FY)1996, 1.1 percent of the direct salary budget of the University of Illinois was dedicated to remediation, whereas 6.5 percent of the direct salary budget of the community colleges in that state was used for remedial services. In FY1995, the percentage of expenditures for remediation in Maryland was 1.2 percent of the total expenditures for the public campuses. In Washington, 7 percent of total expenditures was dedicated to remedial education in 1995–1996. Focusing on the appropriation per full-time equivalent (FTE) student for individual states, the cost to California for remediation is about $2,950 per FTE student and the cost to Florida is about $2,409 (Breneman & Haarlow, 1998).

More recently, Greene (2000) conducted a study of costs of remediation in Michigan, published by the Mackinac Center for Public Policy. He explored a variety of ways to measure costs and extrapolated these measures into national numbers. The spread was enormous, ranging from $773 million to $16.6 billion annually. The number that was comparably calculated to those reported by Breneman was the lower figure of $773 million, which is in the same ballpark as Breneman's estimate. The higher figures added various social costs, which arguably are not the direct cost of remedial programs but, rather, costs to society of failing to educate young people to high standards.

Several factors impede the collecting of reliable data about the costs of remediation:

- Lack of a universally accepted definition of what constitutes remedial education on the part of the academic community
- Wide variation in how "costs" are distributed among the several activities within a college or university
- Difficulty on the part of higher education institutions in supplying precise breakdowns of remediation costs, even if it is understood what functions are to be included in determining the cost of remediation
- Lack of clarity as to whether reported figures reflect expenditures or appropriations
- Uncertainty regarding the age of reported financial data, since states do not compute remediation education costs on a regular basis

Perhaps the most intractable barrier to collecting valid and reliable data on remediation is the tendency of official estimates to understate the extent and cost of remediation (Astin, 1998). This underreporting occurs for a variety of reasons, not the least of which is the perceived damage to the reputation of a college or university. Thus, we can conclude that the costs of remediation are higher than reported. Our estimate is that the figure is probably closer to $2 billion. However, if $2 billion is the actual cost of remediation, or 2 percent of higher education expenditures, that is a relatively modest amount for an activity of such importance to the nation.

The Arkansas Department of Higher Education has conducted a comprehensive study for several years that compares direct and indirect instructional costs of academic programs for the state's public colleges and universities (Arkansas Department of Higher Education, 1998). In 1996–1997, the total cost of remediation in Arkansas colleges and universities was $27 million, approximately 3 percent of the total expenditures. At community colleges, 9 percent of total expenditures was for remedial education, compared to only 2 percent at four-year institutions. The total state subsidy for remedial education was almost $14 million. The state subsidy for community colleges was 59 percent of the total expenditures for remediation, compared to 40 percent at four-year institutions. These data show that although remediation is provided at both four-year and two-year institutions, community colleges commit substantially more resources to it—which is not surprising, given their open admissions policies.

One issue most institutions grapple with is resource allocation: How can the institution utilize limited resources to the greatest benefit? With respect to remediation, what is the cost-benefit of providing remediation? How do the costs of low demand programs, programs with few graduates, compare to remedial education costs, and can resources be better utilized elsewhere? How is the cost per FTE student in academic programs affected by remedial students who are successful and participate in college-level courses? These and other questions can frame the public policy debate regarding the cost of remediation.

## BENEFITS

Research regarding the effectiveness of remedial education programs has been sporadic, typically underfunded, and often inconclusive. For instance, a study of 116 two- and four-year colleges and universities revealed that only a small percentage conducted any systematic evaluation of their remedial education programs (Weissman, Bulakowski, & Jumisco, 1997). Since few states have exit standards for remedial courses, it is unclear whether many states know if their programs work (Crowe, 1998).

Adelman (1999) offers insight into the success of remedial education programs by examining college transcripts from the national high school class of 1982. His study shows an inverse relationship between the extent of students' need for remedial courses and their eventual completion of a degree. This relationship holds true in the more recent data presented in *The Condition of Education 2000* (U.S. Department of Education, 2000). However, these data also show that students who complete one or two remedial courses graduate at rates remarkably similar to those of their peers who take no remedial coursework. For example, the two- or four-year degree completion rate for students who take one remedial course (not mathematics or reading) is fully 98 percent that of their peers who take no remedial courses (see Table 7.1).

Table 7.1
Degree Completion Rates, 1980–1993

| Number/Type of Remedial Courses Taken | 2- or 4-Year Degree Completed | As a % of No Remedial Courses |
|---|---|---|
| None | 56% | – |
| One (not mathematics or reading) | 55 | 98% |
| Two or more (no reading) | 43 | 77 |
| Two or fewer (mathematics only) | 45 | 80 |
| Any remedial reading | 34 | 61 |

*Source*: U.S. Department of Education (2000).

McCabe's recent monograph (2000) provides a good example of the type of empirical research that is needed to help quantify the benefits of remedial programs. A sample of 1,520 students who began remedial programs in 1990 in twenty-five community colleges was surveyed recently to determine the outcome. Of that group, 592 (39 percent) had successfully completed their remedial programs and had gone on to earn a variety of degrees and certificates. Their occupational status was improved, and their incomes were higher as a result. McCabe views the results as clearly indicative of positive payoff to the programs, although he does not attempt to do a rigorous cost-benefit analysis.

In our judgment, further work of this sort will be required to ground the assessment of remediation in hard evidence regarding outcomes. Eventually, studies should allow an institution, or a system of state colleges, to compare the costs of remediation with the benefits accruing to graduates who required such help. Until such studies are done, however, policymakers will have to form judgments of an implicit cost-benefit nature. We believe that most remedial programs would pass that test with flying colors.

## SUPPORT SERVICES

The problems that disadvantaged students face in getting through college are complex. In addition to financial aid and remediation, various types of support services also are available to students. These programs emanate from several sources—the federal and state governments, the colleges and universities themselves, and even corporations and foundations. In many cases, efforts combine several strategies to address the obstacles that these students face.

Research has identified strategies to help students who are at risk of dropping out of college. One of the most commonly cited works on student retention and persistence is Vincent Tinto's *Leaving College* (1987). His model identifies pre-college academic preparation, socioeconomic background, personal goals, academic performance, and campus social interaction as factors that affect a student's decision to enroll and stay in postsecondary education. More recent studies have looked at other specific factors and indicators of success in greater detail, such as faculty-student interaction, financial aid packaging, working while enrolled in school, and attendance patterns (Pascarella & Terenzini, 1991). The following overview describes available student support services, identifies factors influencing student success, and assesses the efficacy of support strategies.

## Federal Efforts

At the federal level, several types of support services are incorporated into various programs and policies. The TRIO programs, sponsored by the U.S. Department of Education, are perhaps the most important initiative to promote student success in college (see Chapter 6 for more on the TRIO programs). Five individual programs comprise TRIO: Upward Bound, Talent Search, Educational Opportunity Centers, Student Support Services, and Ronald E. McNair Postbaccalaureate Achievement. These programs primarily target students from families with income under $24,000, in which neither parent has graduated from college. Overall, the TRIO programs serve students from approximately the sixth to twelfth grade and displaced and underemployed workers, as well as students enrolled in postsecondary education. Over 1,900 TRIO programs currently serve nearly 700,000 lower-income Americans. In FY2001, the TRIO programs were funded at $730 million, an increase of $85 million, or 13 percent, over FY2000 (Burd & Southwick, 2001).

Three TRIO programs provide the majority of support services for college students:

- *Educational Opportunity Centers* Displaced or underemployed workers from lower-income families are given counseling about career and postsecondary options and are directed toward financial aid opportunities.

- *Student Support Services* (SSS) Lower-income students enrolled in postsecondary institutions, which frequently include Upward Bound alumni and disabled students, are given academic counseling, mentoring, tutoring, and remedial instruction needed to ensure degree completion. The FY2001 appropriation bill also authorized additional aid in the form of College Completion Challenge Grants awarded by institutions to students enrolled in SSS projects.

- *McNair Postbaccalaureate Achievement* Research opportunities and faculty mentors are made available to lower-income and minority students enrolled in postsecondary institutions to encourage pursuit of advanced degrees and teaching at the college level.

Directly or indirectly supporting low-income and disadvantaged college students are a variety of other federal programs, such as the Gaining Early Awareness and Readiness for Undergraduate Programs (GEAR-UP). Another example is the College Assistance Migrant Program (CAMP), which provides counseling, tutoring, skills workshops, financial aid stipends, and housing assistance to students who are migratory or seasonal farm workers (or are children of such workers) enrolled in their first year of college.

## State, Institutional, and Private Efforts

Many college-level support programs arose at the grassroots level, predating federal and, in some cases, even state support. Currently, most programs receive financial assistance from a variety of funders, both public and private. States ranging from Massachusetts to California have long subsidized academic counseling, mentoring, and support programs for college students, often through grants to institutions of higher education.

National and local foundations also have contributed funding to develop and expand these college support programs. Other programs, such as the Higher Education Information Center in Boston, offer prospective and current students a wide range of services using funds provided by a diverse set of public and private sources.

## FACTORS AFFECTING STUDENT SUCCESS

### Academic Preparation and Performance

Admissions testing and high school grades have long been tied to college performance and persistence in college (Porter, 1991). However, socioeconomic status and pre-college academic performance are linked through the fact that lower-income students are, in general, more likely to attend lower-quality elementary and secondary schools than students from families with higher incomes. These schools are less likely to offer college preparatory and more demanding curricula, which can have a large effect on students' academic preparation (Institute for Higher Education Policy, 1994). Not surprisingly, grades are probably the greatest influence on a student's chances of receiving a college degree; if a student does not achieve passing grades, he or she will not graduate (Pascarella & Terenzini, 1991). In fact, Pascarella and Terenzini refer to grades as not only strongly related to persistence but also indicative "of successful adaptation to an academic environment" (p. 388).

## Attendance Patterns

Research suggests that delays in enrollment or interruptions in attendance have statistically significant negative effects on the number of years of college completed (Pascarella & Terenzini, 1991). For an individual, leaving school for a period of time may be a necessary step, but in general, the evidence is clear that the chances of success in college are enhanced when attendance occurs in a continuous sequence from beginning to degree completion. Transferring colleges is another form of interrupting attendance, and although the motivation for transfer can often reflect the desire to find a better institutional fit, the number of colleges attended has a small, but significant, negative effect on bachelor's degree attainment (Tinto, 1987; Pascarella & Terenzini, 1991). These findings are particularly important because the tendency for students to attend more than one school is increasing (Adelman, 1999). Among other things, these findings suggest the importance of choosing an initial institution that is a good fit for the student.

Students who attend school part time are also at greater risk for failure to persist to a degree. The increased length of time in school can make completing more difficult. In addition, these students often are under time pressures, impeding contact with faculty and other people on campus. This leads to feelings of isolation on campus and less commitment to one's institution, which, as discussed in the next section, can have a negative effect on degree attainment (Tinto, 1987).

## Social Integration

A student's social integration consists of several components, including student interaction with peer groups, participation in campus activities, interactions with faculty, and advising (Institute for Higher Education Policy, 1994). Being socially integrated on campus leads to student attachment to the institution, which is linked to a higher likelihood of persistence. For example, belonging to a group or organization can strengthen personal bonds with the institution, which—all other things being equal—increases the likelihood of completing a degree. Similarly, both the frequency and quality of students' interactions with peers and faculty are positively associated with persistence (Pascarella & Terenzini, 1991). Faculty interaction seems to have an indirect effect through its positive impact on grades and satisfaction with the institution, which also are strongly linked to persistence to a degree.

Living on campus is consistently one of the most important influences on a student's level of integration. It is not surprising that students who live on campus have significantly more social interaction with peers and faculty and are more likely to be involved in extracurricular activities than are students who must commute to campus. Given the links between social integration and persistence, it follows that living on campus has a statistically significant positive effect on bachelor's degree attainment (Pascarella & Terenzini, 1991).

## Financial Aid and Work

The impact of financial aid on persistence to a bachelor's degree is complex. However, according to the Institute for Higher Education Policy (1994), three important conclusions can be drawn from the research:

- In general, financial aid has a positive impact on persistence;
- Certain types of aid are more likely to have a positive impact than others; and
- The relationship between aid and persistence is not straightforward and is often indirect, especially with respect to lower-income and minority students.

Many studies have established links between financial aid and degree completion, reporting that aid recipients seem to be persisting at least as well, if not better than, non-recipients. Although at first this may not seem to be an impressive conclusion, when one considers that aid is intended to create an equal playing field for economically disadvantaged students, it is perhaps a truly great achievement, given the type of student most likely to receive aid. Even an equalizing effect on persistence between recipients and nonrecipients means that aid is successfully fulfilling its overall objective (Institute for Higher Education Policy, 1994).

Not all types of aid have the same effect on student success, however. Studies show that grants have the largest positive effect, especially when given in significant amounts that are renewable through the years of study

(Washington Higher Education Coordinating Board, 1995). In fact, a study by the U.S. General Accounting Office (1995) found that providing African American and Hispanic students with an extra $1,000 in grant money significantly decreased their probability of dropping out; the findings were even stronger for lower-income students. In contrast, an additional $1,000 in loan aid for lower-income and African American students had the opposite effect, resulting in an increase in the probability of dropping out (see Table 7.2).

In an effort to make ends meet while paying for the ever-rising cost of college, a large number of students work while enrolled. Working while in school, however, does not necessarily have a negative impact on degree completion. Evidence indicates that a work-study job can have a positive effect, whereas the results are more mixed for non–work-study jobs. However, the number of hours the student works must remain at approximately twenty hours a week or less in order for the work-study experience to be a positive one with respect to persistence (Washington Higher Education Coordinating Board, 1995). Many researchers have argued that the positive impact of a work-study job is related to the increased integration to campus life that it provides, whereas a job other than work-study (which is most likely off campus) can have the opposite effect (Pascarella & Terenzini, 1991).

## EVIDENCE OF SUCCESS FROM SUPPORT SERVICES PROGRAMS

Given these key factors affecting student success in college, various programs and policies have been implemented by colleges and universities—often with governmental assistance—to target resources and interventions. Recent studies suggest that many of these programs and policies have been successful in improving students' chances of success in college, although the evaluative evidence is still quite limited.

An evaluation of students participating in the Student Support Services component of the TRIO programs found credible evidence of success (U.S. Department of Education, 1997). The study included a survey of 5,800 SSS participants from 1991–1992, with a three-year follow-up that included a second survey and an analysis of student transcripts. The report indicated several important outcomes of the program:

- The SSS has a positive and statistically significant effect on student outcomes, including grades, credits earned, and retention.
- Students who participated the most in SSS activities, such as peer tutoring, experienced the greatest improvement in outcomes.

**Table 7.2**
Relationship of Financial Aid Packages and Dropout Rates

| Group | Financial Aid Package | Dropout Probability |
|---|---|---|
| Low income students | All students | 15.2% |
| | + $1,000 grant | 13.0 |
| | + $1,000 loan | 15.7 |
| African Americans | All students | 11.4 |
| | + $1,000 grant | 10.7 |
| | + $1,000 loan | 11.6 |
| Hispanics | All students | 17.4 |
| | + $1,000 grant | 15.5 |
| | + $1,000 loan | 15.9 |

Source: U.S. General Accounting Office (1995).

- Peer tutoring, cultural events for students, workshops, and instructional courses exclusively for program participants were the most effective strategies for improving student outcomes.

An analysis of the success of TRIO students at independent colleges and universities indicates similar outcomes (Balz & Esten, 1998). The analysis, which includes data from both the High School and Beyond (1980 to 1992) study and the Beginning Postsecondary Students (1990 to 1994) longitudinal study (both conducted for the National Center for Education Statistics), found that TRIO participants generally performed better in college and remained in school longer than their non-TRIO counterparts of similar income and race or ethnicity. For example, TRIO participants reported higher levels of graduate school enrollment and had higher rates of bachelor's degree attainment than the non-TRIO group.

## ISSUES AND CHALLENGES

Both remediation and support services for college students represent fundamental investment strategies for higher education. The goal of these interventions is to increase the likelihood of success for students who have already taken the important step of applying to college and enrolling.

With regard to remediation, until data are assembled that will permit careful cost-benefit analyses, policymakers will be forced to perform their own calculations based on experience, hunch, and casual observation. We point to McCabe (2000), who discusses the aging of the U.S. population, the growing skill requirements of the labor force, and the enlightened self-interest that should motivate the polity to ensure that all citizens have the means to live productive and successful lives. For the foreseeable future, remedial education will be an essential part of that picture, and therefore we judge the social cost-benefit calculation to be one of enormous payoff, both to the individuals affected and to society at large.

Until compelling evidence is produced that contradicts this view, we argue for maintaining remedial options as an important part of the post-secondary educational system. In particular, we should not allow the critics of public schooling to undermine the important continuing role of remedial programs, nor should we allow the understandable desire of college leaders to seek prestige for their schools to have that same effect. This is a clear case of elite opinion being out of step with the common sense of ordinary citizens, who highly value educational second chances.

Similarly, student support services provide a combination of strategies that increase the likelihood of success for educationally disadvantaged populations. Programs that target the key variables associated with student success, such as the SSS component of the Federal TRIO program, are an essential part of the overall strategy of equalizing educational opportunity. As with remediation, policymakers need more and better information about the specific investments in student support that lead to persistence and educational goal attainment in college. Even with the limited evidence available, it is clear that these programs provide tangible benefits associated with increasing student success. Investment in these programs at a level sufficient to reach all eligible populations should therefore be a critical element of national strategies to enhance human capital. Failing to make these investments will surely lead to a reduction in both the public and the private benefits associated with college education.

## REFERENCES

Adelman, C. (1999). *Answers in the tool box: Academic intensity, attendance patterns, and bachelor's degree attainment.* Washington, DC: U.S. Department of Education, Office of Educational Research and Improvement.

Arkansas Department of Higher Education. (1998). *Arkansas academic cost accounting.* Little Rock: Author.

Astin, A. (1998, June). Higher education and civic responsibility. Paper presented at the American Council on Education's Conference on Civic Roles and Responsibilities, Washington, DC.

Balz, F. J., & Esten, M. R. (1998, fall). Fulfilling private dreams, serving public priorities: An analysis of TRIO students' success at independent colleges and universities. *Journal of Negro Education, 67*(4), 333–45.

Breneman, D. W. (1998). Remediation in higher education: Its extent and cost. In D. Ravitch (ed.), *Brookings papers on education policy* (pp. 359–83). Washington, DC: Brookings Institution Press.

Breneman, D. W., & Haarlow, W. N. (1998, July). *Remedial education: Costs and consequences from remediation in higher education: A symposium*. Washington, DC: Fordham Foundation.

Burd, S., & Southwick, R. (2001, January 5). Student aid and NIH gain in budget deal. *Chronicle of Higher Education*, A36.

Crowe, E.. (1998). *Statewide remedial education policies*. Denver, CO: State Higher Education Executive Officers.

Greene, J. P. (2000). *The cost of remedial education: How much Michigan pays when students fail to learn basic skills*. Midland, MI: Mackinac Center for Public Policy.

Ignash, J. (1997, winter). Who should provide postsecondary remedial/developmental Education? In J. Ignash (ed), *Implementing effective policies for remedial and developmental education*. New Directions for Community Colleges (100). San Francisco, CA: Jossey-Bass Publishers.

Institute for Higher Education Policy and Educational Resources Institute. (1994). *The next step: Student aid for student success*. Washington, DC: Author.

Maryland Higher Education Commission. (1996). *A study of remedial education at Maryland public campuses*. Annapolis: Maryland Higher Education Commission.

Mazzeo, C. (2001). Stakes for students: Agenda-setting and remedial education. Unpublished manuscript. New York: School of Public Affairs, Baruch College/City University of New York.

McCabe, R. H. (2000). *No one to waste: A report to public decision-makers and community college leaders*. Washington, DC: Community College Press.

Pascarella, E. T., & Terenzini, P. T. (1991). *How college affects students*. San Francisco, CA: Jossey-Bass Publishers.

Payne, E., & Lyman, B. (1998). *Issues affecting the definition of developmental education*. National Association of Developmental Education. (http://www.umkc.edu/cad/nade/index.htm).

Porter, O. (1991, summer). Where do we go from here: Looking beyond student aid and access to persistence. In J. Merisotis (ed.), *New Directions for Higher Education* (74), pp. 75–90. San Francisco: Jossey-Bass Publishers.

Ruppert, S. (1996). *The politics of remedy: State legislative views on higher education*. Washington, DC: National Education Association.

Saxon, P., & Boylan, H. (2000). Issues in community college remedial education. Working Manuscript. Miami, FL: League for Innovation in the Community College.

Tinto, V. (1987). *Leaving college: Rethinking the causes and cures of student attrition*. Chicago: University of Chicago Press.

Trombley, W., Doyle, W., & Davis, J. (1998, summer). The remedial controversy. *National Crosstalk*, 6(3), 2.

U.S. Department of Education, National Center for Education Statistics. (1996). *Remedial education at higher education institutions in fall 1995*. NCES 97-584. Washington, DC: Author.

U.S. Department of Education, National Center for Education Statistics. (2000). *The condition of education, 2000*. NCES 2000-062. Washington, DC: Author.

U.S. Department of Education, Planning and Evaluation Service. (1997). *National study of student support services: Third year longitudinal study results*. Washington, DC: Author.

U.S. General Accounting Office. (1995). *Higher education: Restructuring student aid could reduce low-income student dropout rate*. HEHS-95-48. Washington, DC: Author.

Washington Higher Education Coordinating Board. (1995, March). *The impact of student financial aid on persistence: A summary of national research and literature*. Olympia, WA: Author.

Weissman, J., Bulakowski, C., & Jumisco, M. (1997, winter). Using research to evaluate developmental education programs and policies." In J. Ignash (ed.), *New Directions for Community Colleges* (100), pp. 73–80. San Francisco, CA: Jossey-Bass Publishers.

# PART IV

## The Future

# CHAPTER 8

# The Demographic Window of Opportunity: College Access and Diversity in the New Century

*Anthony P. Carnevale and Richard A. Fry*

The first fifteen years of the new century present unprecedented challenges and new opportunities for achieving access and equity in higher education. While no one can predict the future precisely, demographic trends and economic projections suggest the shape of things to come. Demography is the most powerful determinant of the future of higher education. The number of 18- to 24-year-olds, the traditional college-age population, will increase more than 16 percent by 2015, from 26 million to 30 million youth. Assuming that the new youth cohort will be at least as well prepared as current high school graduates, the number of qualified postsecondary students will grow by as much as 1.6 million. In addition, a likely influx of 1 million "nontraditional" students could bring the total estimated new enrollment figure to 2.6 million (Carnevale & Fry, 2000).

This chapter explores the demographic forecast for the next fifteen years and the implications of these projections. We look first at the anticipated growth of minority and immigrant groups, the population trends across states, and the probable college-readiness of the new cohort. Based on our estimates, we predict the impact that this cohort will have on the labor market, the cost of educating more students, and equity in access to higher education. Our analysis delves into the policy challenges presented by possible misinterpretation of statistics on higher education and the difficulties that states and the federal government will face in providing adequate financial aid for increased numbers of needy students. In conclusion, our discussion illuminates the potential effects of increased costs and policy changes on lower-income and minority college-bound youth.

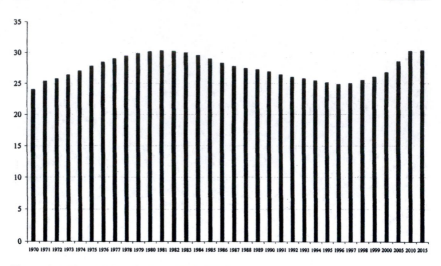

*Figure 8.1 18 to 24 Population, 1970–2015*

Source: U.S. Department of Education (2001) and U.S. Census Bureau (2001).

## THE LOOMING FUTURE: "GENERATION Y" REACHES COLLEGE AGE

United States Census Bureau projections indicate that higher education is facing a major expansion in demand for seats in America's college class-rooms over the next ten years. The size of its core client base of 18- to 24-year-olds is expected to rise from 26 million today to over 30 million by 2010, and to remain above 30 million through 2015 (see Figure 8.1).In 2001, about 37 percent of 18- to 24-year-olds were enrolled in college.

The imminent rise in the traditional college-age population reflects the maturation of "Generation Y," the "baby boom echo" comprised of those born between 1982 and 1997, as well as increased immigration to the United States since 1980. The heart of Generation Y, those born between 1989 and 1993, will reach age 18 between 2007 and 2011, and the last of the Generation Y bulge will hit age 24 in 2017.

### Racial and Ethnic Characteristics

Table 8.1 reveals the importance of immigration in determining the characteristics of students who will be participating in higher education over the next fifteen years. Today, one in five U.S. children is the child of

Table 8.1
Projected National Growth in the Traditional College-Age Population,
2000–2015 (millions)

| | Total | Hispanic | Non-Hispanic Asian/Pacific Islander | Black | Non-Hispanic Native American | White |
|---|---|---|---|---|---|---|
| 2000 | 26.26 | 3.68 | 1.08 | 3.75 | 0.24 | 17.51 |
| 2015 | 30.52 | 5.76 | 1.77 | 4.43 | 0.27 | 18.29 |
| Absolute Increase | 4.26 | 2.08 | 0.69 | 0.68 | 0.03 | 0.78 |
| Percent Increase | 16.2% | 56.4% | 63.8% | 18.1% | 14.8% | 4.4% |
| Share of Growth (in %) | | 48.8% | 16.2% | 16.0% | 0.8% | 18.2% |

*Source:* Campbell (1996).

an immigrant (Urban Institute, 2000). Fully half of Californians under age 18 are first- or second-generation Americans. It is these children who will fuel the growth of higher education in the coming years.

The good news is that roughly 80 percent of the new students who are qualified for college will be minorities. As many as 400,000 new Hispanics and 200,000 new African Americans are likely to be attending college by 2015. Whereas white youth are projected to remain the majority, this group is expected to expand by only about 4.4 percent (see Table 8.1). Minority 18- to 24-year-olds will grow by approximately 3.5 million, or about 40 percent. Reflecting the influence of recent U.S. immigration, the numbers of Asian and Hispanic youth should rise by about 64 and 56 percent, respectively. Together, these groups will account for 2.8 million of the 4 million plus growth in the traditional college-age population. Whether or not the boom in demographics will result in increases in college enrollments during the next decade will largely depend on our success in fully integrating the nation's Hispanic and other minority and immigrant youth into the ranks of high school graduates.

The demographic forces already in place ensure a surge in students, especially minority students, ready for college. We could increase access to college even more, especially for minority and lower-income students, if we harnessed this demographic momentum to policies that promote greater equality in the opportunity to learn. The first fifteen years of the new century could result in a historic rise not only in the sheer numbers of qualified college-age students but in their diversity as well.

# Table 8.2
## Projected State Growth in the Traditional College-Age Population, 2000 to 2015

| State | 2000 | 2015 | 2000 to 2015 Increase | % Increase |
|---|---|---|---|---|
| California | 3,131,470 | 4,718,293 | 1,586,823 | 50.7 |
| Texas | 2,128,779 | 2,639,950 | 511,171 | 24.0 |
| New York | 1,629,083 | 1,958,481 | 329,398 | 20.2 |
| Florida | 1,253,105 | 1,537,390 | 284,285 | 22.7 |
| Georgia | 794,350 | 938,418 | 144,068 | 18.1 |
| Massachusetts | 548,967 | 681,404 | 132,437 | 24.1 |
| Virginia | 661,244 | 792,680 | 131,436 | 19.9 |
| New Jersey | 698,763 | 818,485 | 119,722 | 17.1 |
| Illinois | 1,169,289 | 1,287,962 | 118,673 | 10.1 |
| North Carolina | 724,072 | 839,033 | 114,961 | 15.9 |
| Arizona | 466,273 | 564,818 | 98,545 | 21.1 |
| Maryland | 467,530 | 564,931 | 97,401 | 20.8 |
| Washington | 557,446 | 637,519 | 80,073 | 14.4 |
| Tennessee | 545,289 | 598,780 | 53,491 | 9.8 |
| Connecticut | 275,133 | 327,511 | 52,378 | 19.0 |
| Pennsylvania | 1,066,220 | 1,116,862 | 50,642 | 4.7 |
| South Carolina | 367,713 | 416,822 | 49,109 | 13.4 |
| Colorado | 416,357 | 459,887 | 43,530 | 10.5 |
| Alabama | 432,573 | 474,222 | 41,649 | 9.6 |
| Hawaii | 120,951 | 156,012 | 35,061 | 29.0 |
| New Mexico | 186,851 | 220,384 | 33,533 | 17.9 |
| Louisiana | 473,148 | 502,218 | 29,070 | 6.1 |
| District of Col. | 54,980 | 80,817 | 25,837 | 47.0 |
| Rhode Island | 85,792 | 108,156 | 22,364 | 26.1 |
| Utah | 296,943 | 317,042 | 20,099 | 6.8 |
| Oklahoma | 338,354 | 358,398 | 20,044 | 5.9 |
| Nevada | 168,764 | 187,216 | 18,452 | 10.9 |
| Indiana | 596,796 | 614,658 | 17,862 | 3.0 |
| Missouri | 537,867 | 555,426 | 17,559 | 3.3 |
| Oregon | 317,317 | 333,613 | 16,296 | 5.1 |
| Alaska | 72,208 | 87,809 | 15,601 | 21.6 |
| Kansas | 269,625 | 284,748 | 15,123 | 5.6 |
| New Hampshire | 109,400 | 122,551 | 13,151 | 12.0 |
| Michigan | 924,131 | 936,107 | 11,976 | 1.3 |
| Delaware | 71,873 | 80,660 | 8,787 | 12.2 |
| Vermont | 56,454 | 59,151 | 2,697 | 4.8 |
| Wyoming | 56,696 | 58,388 | 1,692 | 3.0 |
| Mississippi | 293,424 | 294,203 | 779 | 0.3 |
| Nebraska | 174,815 | 173,088 | -1,727 | -1.0 |
| Maine | 110,770 | 108,451 | -2,319 | -2.1 |
| North Dakota | 73,010 | 70,533 | -2,477 | -3.4 |
| Idaho | 148,366 | 145,439 | -2,927 | -2.0 |
| Arkansas | 252,808 | 249,447 | -3,361 | -1.3 |

*(Continued)*

**Table 8.2** *(continued)*

| | | | | |
|---|---|---|---|---|
| Ohio | 1,086,624 | 1,083,205 | -3,419 | -0.3 |
| South Dakota | 82,286 | 75,320 | -6,966 | -8.5 |
| Montana | 92,945 | 84,416 | -8,529 | -9.2 |
| Minnesota | 485,566 | 476,195 | -9,371 | -1.9 |
| Kentucky | 394,017 | 384,071 | -9,946 | -2.5 |
| Wisconsin | 530,041 | 513,632 | -16,409 | -3.1 |
| West Virginia | 174,053 | 153,473 | -20,580 | -11.8 |
| Iowa | 288,069 | 267,436 | -20,633 | -7.2 |

*Source:* Campbell (1996).

## Demographic Trends by State

Most youth attend college in their home state, and thus national figures distort the issues that most states will face in accommodating future students. Indeed, the bulk of the projected increase in college-age youth—an estimated 67 percent—is concentrated in five states: California, Texas, New York, Florida, and Georgia (Table 8.2). With the exception of Georgia, all these states are experiencing international immigration and burgeoning Latino youth populations. Thirteen states in the north central and northeast United States are expected to experience declines in their traditional college-age populations. Indeed, because most of the growth is concentrated in twelve coastal states, thirty-nine states will each see an increase of less than 83,000 in the 18- to 24-year-old population (the increase each state would experience if the 4.3 million anticipated students were distributed evenly). Much of the interior of the United States (except Illinois) will not experience significant growth in college-age youth. Given the very uneven nature of the expansion, a handful of states will be under extraordinary pressure to accommodate their ballooning college enrollments.

## Academic Preparation

The level of academic skills that the new cohort of college-age youth will have is an important factor in assessing the impact of the boom on educational diversity. One of the key determinants of college access is academic preparation. Although high school graduation is a prerequisite to timely entry into college, graduation alone is not sufficient. Among high school graduates, those who are strongly academically prepared to do college-level work are much more likely to enter college than are youth who are weakly prepared. Because of the growing proportion of minority children and the well-known gaps between minority and white children on achievement tests, some have expressed concerns that Generation Y may be less academically prepared to enter college and succeed than earlier generations.

Since the bulk of Generation Y has not yet reached high school, it is impossible to report conclusively on the skills of this group. However, the National Assessment of Educational Progress (NAEP), often referred to as the "nation's report card," provides the most reliable indicator of the academic skills of our nation's youth. The latest NAEP round of testing, conducted in 1999, provides results on mathematics, reading, and science abilities for 9-year-olds, students squarely in Generation Y. Nine-year-olds in 1999 performed no worse, on average, in any subject area than earlier cohorts, and they performed significantly better in all subject areas than their baby-boomer parents, who took the assessment as 9-year-olds in the early 1970s (Table 8.3). It is early yet, and clearly there is much to be learned between age 9 and high school graduation. However, the available evidence suggests that the upcoming cohort of 18- to 24-year-olds will be at least as well prepared for college as previous generations.

Particularly, early test results from the NAEP and other sources suggest that the share of minority students ready for college will stay the same or grow slightly. The new cohorts will be at least as well prepared as previous minority cohorts. This means that as minority students grow as a proportion of 18- to 24-year-olds, the number of college-qualified minorities should increase substantially.

## IMPLICATIONS FOR THE FUTURE

Given what we know about the size, composition, and academic preparation of Generation Y, we can assess the impact of this cohort on the labor market, the costs to higher education, and the potential of these shifting demographics for promoting equity in access to higher education.

### The Labor Market

The shape of the economy is a near certainty in the new century. We know from the evidence of the past few decades that people need college to compete in the new knowledge economy. Prime-age jobs that require at least some college have increased from 20 percent in 1959 to 56 percent

Table 8.3
NEAP Academic Progress for Nine-Year-Olds

| Year | Math | Year | Reading | Year | Science |
|------|------|------|---------|------|---------|
| 1973 | 219  | 1971 | 208     | 1970 | 225     |
| 1978 | 219  | 1975 | 210     | 1973 | 220     |
| 1982 | 219  | 1980 | 215     | 1977 | 220     |
| 1986 | 222  | 1984 | 211     | 1982 | 221     |
| 1990 | 230  | 1988 | 212     | 1986 | 224     |
| 1992 | 230  | 1990 | 209     | 1990 | 229     |
| 1994 | 231  | 1992 | 211     | 1992 | 231     |
| 1996 | 231  | 1994 | 211     | 1994 | 231     |
| 1999 | 232  | 1996 | 212     | 1996 | 230     |
|      |      | 1999 | 212     | 1999 | 229     |

Note: Scores are mean scores, scale of 0 to 500.
Source: Campbell, Hambo, & Mazzeo (2000).

in 1997 (Carnevale, 1999). Access to college has become the gateway to our individual hopes and aspirations, as well as the ante for earning a family wage.

In the knowledge economy, our ability to produce college-level workers will determine our overall economic competitiveness and ensure individual economic opportunity for all Americans. Also, considerable macroeconomic benefits can accrue from more minorities and lower-income students on campus. For instance, if we could equalize majority and minority college-level attainment, we would add more than $230 billion to the nation's wealth, providing an additional $80 billion in new tax revenues (Carnevale, 1999). We would also reduce the share of Hispanic and African American families subsisting on officially "inadequate" incomes from 41 to 21 percent and from 33 to 24 percent, respectively, moving us closer to realizing our egalitarian goals (Carnevale, 1999).

## The Cost to Higher Education

The future costs of these demographic shifts make celebrations premature. The surge in the 18- to 24-year-olds seems to signal overall growth in the higher education sector and greater access for minorities and lower-income students, yet the effect of demography on higher education costs suggests a more complex scenario.

Internal Educational Testing Service tabulations suggest that the influx of new students could easily add at least $19 billion in new costs, inhibiting our ability to capitalize on the demographic momentum of college-age students, especially those from minority and lower-income families. In addition to the added costs for infrastructure and technology upgrades, it is increasingly apparent that higher education needs to invest more in outreach, admissions, and supportive services. More resources will be required to connect campuses to communities, to coordinate college curricula with the K–12 education system, and to gear college studies to career opportunities. Moreover, new resources will be needed to install admissions procedures that link colleges to families, especially in an era in which affirmative action is under attack and colleges and universities struggle to find more sophisticated ways to assess merit and promote diversity on campus.

It is doubtful that a "reengineering" of higher education in order to serve more students at lower cost will suffice or come in time for the flood of new students who began arriving on college campuses in 1997. There are few indications that the education industry is likely to become more productive in the near future as a result of organizational or other structural changes. Nor is it likely that technology will save us by creating "virtual universities" for new students. In general, experience in other service industries shows that technology adds value more than it reduces cost. The most powerful long-term effects are, not reduced costs, but benefits such as quality, variety, customization, convenience, speed, and novelty; in addition, the initial investments are expensive. Neither "reengineering" nor technology can offer a "quick fix" solution for the cost pressures that higher education will experience in the future.

These demographic shifts represent an unprecedented opportunity for higher education and for traditional- and non-traditional-age college students. However, the rising costs associated with a larger and more diverse student body cannot be ignored. Cost squeezes create an environment in which support for lower-income and minority students might be cut, undermining the potential for increased access to and diversity in higher education.

## Equity

Our postsecondary education system is the high water mark in the history of human learning, both because of its quality and because of its accessibility. However, our record on demographic and income diversity, as well as on persistence and graduation, is not keeping up with our overall investments. For instance, since 1971, spending for higher education has increased from $8,500 to $10,500 per student (in constant dollars), but the percentage of students who complete their bachelor's degree has fallen from 50 percent to 46 percent (U.S. Department of Education, 2001). The increased numbers of minorities in the traditional college-age population represent an opportunity to promote equity not only in higher education but also in our society as a whole. The first decades of the new century will shape the future of higher education. We must decide if the costs implicit in the demographic shift are worth the benefits of potential growth in minority enrollment, equity, and ultimately, economic prosperity.

## POLICY ISSUES AND IMPLICATIONS

### Avoiding the Diversity Illusion

As a result of these caveats, the increase in access to higher education in general and for minorities and lower-income students in particular could emerge as more apparent than real. The surge in the 18- to 24-year-olds through 2015 ensures larger enrollments, but not a larger proportion of 18- to 24-year-olds enrolled, which is the true measure of access. Moreover, if a smaller share of a larger pool take college admissions exams, apply, and enroll, admission test scores and college performance are likely to improve. Colleges will be able to admit a more highly qualified minority freshman class, whose subsequent grades and graduation rates will rise relative to previous freshman cohorts from minority families. Thus, the gains in enrollment and performance could create a demographic illusion of broadened access, fueling false optimism about our progress in providing an equal opportunity to learn. In fact, under this scenario increasing minority enrollments, academic performance, and graduation rates could reflect no progress at all, or even a decline in minority access to higher education as measured against the underlying demographic base. Even if our projected massive increase of 1.2 million minority youth on campus materializes, the share of Hispanic and African American 18- to 24-year-olds might fall short of its current proportion by 8 and 3 percentage points, respectively.

### Challenges for States

There may be as many as 1.6 million new youth ready to go to college by 2015, but it is not clear that we can afford them. Far from being a revenue windfall, accommodating an additional 1 to 2 million college students will severely strain state budgets and the charity of contributors to higher education. Higher education is a subsidized endeavor; with the exception of students enrolled in for-profit colleges and universities, few college students and their families pay the full amount of their educational costs. The typical college student and his or her family pay $3,800 for an education that costs $12,000 per year to provide and therefore receives a $8,200 subsidy (Winston, 1999).

At present, states, the federal government, families, and endowments pay 35, 21, 22, and 22 percent, respectively, of higher education costs (McPherson & Shapiro, 1998). An additional 1.6 million students could cost these four participating groups more than $19 billion per year. If current funding patterns hold, states would have to come up with more than $6 billion, or roughly one-third of the money, at a time when they are steadily reducing their share of higher education funding. If the states are unable or unwilling to pay their current share, it is unlikely that endowments or federal aid will grow sufficiently to make up the difference necessary to provide seats for all of the 1 to 2 million new students.

The new education funds will be difficult to find, especially given the competing demands for establishing a universal preschool system, improving standards in elementary and secondary education, and creating opportunities for lifelong learning (and this list does not include non-educational priorities putting demands on state budgets). To make up the shortfall, students and families will have to shoulder the additional burden by paying higher tuition and fees at a time when Americans are already alarmed by rising college costs.

To some extent, the public reaction to increasing college costs is unwarranted. In surveys, the public consistently overstates the expense of college and understates the availability of financial aid, in part because of a media focus on high-priced institutions (Ikenberry & Hartle, 1998). College is still a very good deal, with baccalaureate degrees returning from eight to ten times their cost in additional lifetime earnings. However, there is a more complex reality underlying the public concern about college financing. College costs have more than doubled in real dollars since the 1970s, whereas median-family income has risen by less than 25 percent over the same period. In addition, family budgets have been hit by increasing costs for food, housing, and consumer durables (e.g., cars), as well as by higher taxes, especially for supporting a growing population of retirees. As a result, increasing college costs, though not substantial compared to benefits, are experienced by families as a reduction in disposable income, a drain on savings, or a damper on future disposable income as a result of educational loan obligations. A limited number of choices are available to families facing higher costs for college as the glut of new students reach their majority. Families can spend more of their current or fu-

**Table 8.4**
**1995–1996 Undergraduates Receiving Grant Aid**

|  | Any Grant | Federal Grant | State Grant | Institutional Grant |
|---|---|---|---|---|
| | Percentage of Undergraduates Receiving Grants | | | |
| Asian Pacific/Islander | 36% | 23% | 11% | 18% |
| Hispanic | 47 | 36 | 11 | 15 |
| Black | 53 | 38 | 14 | 14 |
| White | 35 | 17 | 10 | 14 |
| | Average Amount for Those Receiving Grants | | | |
| Asian Pacific/Islander | $4,144 | $1,929 | $2,423 | $3,646 |
| Hispanic | 2,407 | 1,741 | 1,559 | 1,830 |
| Black | 2,619 | 1,715 | 1,449 | 2,746 |
| White | 2,669 | 1,587 | 1,517 | 3,082 |

*Source:* Berkner (1998).

ture discretionary income, use more of their savings, or pay higher taxes to expand government subsidies.

## Challenges for the Federal Government

Although lack of precise knowledge of future family incomes limits our understanding of the demands that the new cohort of students will make on the federal funding sources, it is possible to draw some conclusions based on current demographics and student aid patterns. If funding patterns remain stable, demands for grant assistance are likely to climb steeply. It is not simply a matter of the large size of the Generation Y cohort. College students will increasingly be minority students, and largely because of their lower family incomes, minority college students tend to make greater use of grant assistance, particularly federal grant assistance (Table 8.4). Hispanic and African American undergraduates receive grant aid awards that are, on average, about the same dollar amounts as those received by white undergraduates. But whereas 17 percent of white undergraduates receive federal grant assistance, more than one-third of Hispanic and black undergraduates receives such aid.

Table 8.5 shows the estimated impact of future increases in the number of college students on federal grant assistance. By 2010, the traditional college-age population is projected to increase by about 3.9 million youth. Based on current undergraduate enrollment, the number of Hispanic,

Table 8.5
Simulated Increase in Undergraduate Federal Grant Aid Recipients,
2000–2010

| | | | Non-Hispanic | | |
| --- | --- | --- | --- | --- | --- |
| | Total* | Hispanic | Asian/ Pacific Islander | Black | White |
| 2000 18-to-24 population | 26,258,600 | 3,678,779 | 1,079,975 | 3,751,076 | 17,510,127 |
| 2010 18-to-24 population | 30,138,019 | 5,101,130 | 1,521,118 | 4,354,037 | 18,879,802 |
| Absolute population increase | 3,879,419 | 1,442,351 | 441,143 | 602,961 | 1,369,675 |
| % enrolled as undergraduates | | 19.4% | 51.1% | 28.4% | 37.9% |
| Absolute undergrad. increase | | 275,259 | 225,511 | 171,256 | 519,193 |
| % obtaining federal grant aid | | 36% | 23% | 38% | 17% |
| Increase in federal grant aid recipients | | 99,093 | 51,868 | 65,077 | 88,263 |

Source: Authors' calculations.
*Total includes Native Americans.

Asian, black, and white undergraduates might be expected to increase by
275,000, 225,000, 175,000, and 525,000, respectively. If current usage patterns hold steady, the number of undergraduates receiving federal grants
could increase by around 300,000 awardees, which will result in greater demand for Pell Grants (see Chapter 1).

## Impact on Lower-Income and Minority Students

Lower-income students, especially lower-income minority students, will
be the hardest hit by the combined effects of cost pressures and trends in
student aid policies. Since the early 1970s, median incomes for families in
the bottom quintile not only have not risen as fast as college costs, but
have actually declined in constant dollars (Mayer, 1997). The differences
between the top and bottom of the income distribution have also widened
substantially. In addition, the real value of need-based student aid has fallen
far behind the increase in college costs, especially for lower-income families. We know that enrollments of college-age youth from lower-income
families are more sensitive than youth from middle- and upper-income families to increases in college costs (see Chapter 2). One study, for instance,
shows that for every $1,000 increase in the cost of community college,
lower-income enrollments decline by 6 percent (Kane, 1995). Prices also
affect the ability of lower-income students to attend more selective schools.
These students are highly concentrated in the less selective schools. Cur-

rently, only 8 percent of students from families in the bottom quintile who go to four-year schools attend the 146 most selective colleges (Barron's, 2000).

Recent shifts in policy have not favored lower-income students. Federal financial aid policy has gravitated toward middle-income students since the passage of the Middle Income Student Assistance Act in the Carter years (see Chapter 3). Loan volumes are more than five times those of grants, and lower-income families are more reluctant to take on additional debt. The recent shift to tax-based aid in the form of credits and deductions also favors higher-income families, who are better situated to take advantage of tax credits and deductions. State and institutional aid programs are increasingly "merit-based," to the benefit of middle-income families (see Chapters 4 and 5).

Whatever harms lower-income families harms minorities most. Minorities are most highly concentrated in lower-income families. More than 40 percent of Hispanic families and 34 percent of African American families have officially "inadequate" incomes, according to the U.S. Department of Labor, compared to less than 15 percent of white families (Carnevale, 1999). Reflecting their lower family resources, minority undergraduates are more dependent on need-based aid. Currently, about 17 percent of white students receive federal need-based grants, compared with 38 and 36 percent of black and Hispanic students, respectively (Table 8.4). The lack of resources also gives minority families fewer choices. Among students who are in college, only 34 percent of African Americans and 36 percent of Hispanics attend the most selective 1,400 four-year colleges out of the nation's roughly 3,000 two-year and four-year colleges (Carnevale, 1999). More than half of Hispanic students attend community colleges.

## CONCLUSION: BALANCING EDUCATIONAL, CULTURAL, AND ECONOMIC ROLES

The knowledge economy increases the importance of higher education to the nation's overall competitive standing and to the career prospects of individuals. The heightened economic importance of postsecondary education, in combination with the inevitable cost squeeze, will, over the next twenty years, raise fundamental questions about the purposes of higher education, forcing choices among its economic, educational, and cultural roles. The obvious concern is that the growing economic and vocational value of higher education may result in a devaluation and diminution of its academic and cultural roles—critical elements of a participatory political system and an individualistic culture. At the same time, higher education cannot fulfill its cultural and academic missions without paying attention to its economic role. Ours is a society based on work. Those who cannot get and keep a good job are unlikely to participate fully in family and community life. Good jobs create good neighbors and autonomous citizens. Access to higher education has become the prerequisite for a good job.

Future demographic shifts represent an unprecedented opportunity for our nation to maximize the potential of higher education. These changes will no doubt bring challenges in the form of increased costs and shifting priorities. However, rightly understood and courageously confronted, they can also serve to decrease inequities and better the lives of lower-income and minority students while at the same time increasing economic prosperity for the nation as a whole. The wave of new students is beginning to crest; we need to swim with it, not against it.

## REFERENCES

Barron's Educational Services. (2000). *Barron's students' #1 choice: Profiles of American colleges, 23rd edition.* Hauppauge, NY: Author.

Berkner, L. (1998). *Student financing of undergraduate education: 1995–96.* NCES 98-076. Washington, DC: U.S. Department of Education, National Center for Education Statistics.

Campbell, J. R., Hambo, C. M., & Mazzeo, J. (2000). *NAEP 1999 trends in academic progress: Three decades of student performance.* NCES 2000–469. Washington, DC: U.S. Department of Education, National Center for Education Statistics.

Campbell, P. D. (1996). Population projections for states—by age, sex, race, and Hispanic origin, 1995–2005. PPL-47. Washington, DC: U.S. Bureau of the Census.

Carnevale, A. (1999). *Education = success: Empowering Hispanic youth and adults.* Educational Testing Service Leadership 2000 Series. Princeton, NJ: Educational Testing Service.

Carnevale, A., & Fry, R. A. (2000). *Crossing the great divide: Can we achieve equity when Generation Y goes to college?* Educational Testing Service Leadership 2000 Series. Princeton, NJ: Educational Testing Service.

Getz, M., & Siegfried, J. J. (1991). Costs and productivity in American colleges and universities. In C. T. Clotfelter et al. (eds.), *Economic challenges in higher education* (pp. 261–392). Chicago: University of Chicago Press.

Ikenberry, S. O., & Hartle, T. W. (1998). *Too little knowledge is a dangerous thing: What the public thinks about paying for college.* Washington, DC: American Council on Education.

Kane, Thomas J. (1995, July). *Rising public college tuition and college entry: How well do public subsidies promote access to college?* (NBER Working Paper No. 5164). Cambridge, MA: National Bureau of Economic Research.

Mayer, Susan E. (1997). Trends in the economic well-being and life chances of America's children. In G. J. Duncan & J. Brooks-Gunn (eds.), *The consequences of growing up poor* (pp. 49–69). New York: Russell Sage.

McPherson, Michael S. & Morton Owen Schapiro. (1998). *The student aid game: Meeting need and rewarding talent in American higher education.* Princeton, NJ: Princeton University Press.

Urban Institute. (2000, September 2). One in five U.S. children are children of immigrants. *Check points: Data releases on economic and social issues* (http://www.urban.org/ news/press/CP_000911.html). Washington, DC: Author.

U.S. Census Bureau. (2001). National population projections summary files (http://www.census.gov/population/www/projections/natsum-T3.html). Washington, DC: Author.

U.S. Department of Education, National Center for Education Statistics. (2001). *Digest of education statistics, 2000.* NCES 2001–034. Washington, DC: Author.

Winston, Gordon C. (1999). Subsidies, hierarchy and peers: The awkward economics of higher education. *Journal of Economic Perspectives, 13*(1), 13–36.

# CHAPTER

## Policy Priorities and Political Realities

### A. Clayton Spencer

A s outlined in the Preface, this book builds on a report, *Access De-nied: Restoring the Nation's Commitment to Equal Educational Op-portunity*, prepared early in the Bush presidency by the Advisory Committee on Student Financial Assistance (2001). Both studies present a picture of broad, but unequal, access to higher education, with a great deal of the inequity attributable to financial factors.

Notwithstanding an increased emphasis in the public policy domain on problems of academic preparation among low-income students, *Access Denied* and other studies have demonstrated that much of the inequity in par-ticipation, persistence, and degree completion throughout the educational pipeline can be explained in financial terms alone. Unmet financial need—the gap between a student's total educational expenses and available funds from all sources—creates for many students a significant barrier to gaining entrance to, staying in, and completing their chosen courses of study within our institutions of higher education.

The good news is that meeting financial need through increased grant support is a straightforward mechanism that has repeatedly been shown to work. The bad news, as the foregoing chapters have detailed, is that at-tention and funding at every level—federal, state, and institutional—have strayed from the goal of increasing access to higher education by provid-ing grant support to students who do not quite have the funds to attend. Instead, we spent the decade of the 1980s cutting grant funds and ex-panding the availability of, and student dependence on, loans. And we spent the decade of the 1990s invoking the language of access while systematically privileging, in policy and in funding, the broad middle-class concern with affordability. We have enacted massive new tuition tax credits—more on an annual basis than we spend on all federal student aid grants put together[1]—which are broadly popular, but whose effect in ensuring access to higher education is, at best, so far largely unmeasured. States and institutions have likewise targeted new money disproportionately on programs aimed at merit—and thus also disproportionately on middle- and upper-middle-class students.

The goal of removing financial barriers to college attendance thus continues to elude us. At a time when education is more important than ever to the economy and well-being of the nation and of individuals, large gaps remain in the participation and degree completion rates of students from different income categories. Given challenging demographics and the financial pressures on colleges, students, and families alike, these gaps will increase unless we direct focused attention and meaningful resources toward equalizing access to higher education and fostering greater success among those who enter.

As we make our way through the first years of this new century and look toward the next reauthorization of the Higher Education Act, scheduled for 2003, the crucial question is whether we can agree on and build public and political support for coherent policy goals and effective means of achieving them. This concluding chapter considers this question from the point of view of federal policymaking and the political context that frames it. The suggestion is not that federal policy is the sole or even the most significant contributor to access. Certainly students, families, states, and institutions themselves shoulder a far greater proportion of the costs of education in the United States. But, for two reasons, the federal policy domain provides a particularly illuminating perspective on the question of access and whether and how we are likely to improve it. First, the goal of access is most concentrated and easy to isolate for analysis at the federal level. Second, considering the political context and practical constraints of policymaking at the federal level requires that one understand the national context of the debate about education and where it fits with respect to national priorities.

With this context in mind, this chapter will (1) identify a set of policy priorities that constitute the important goals in a legislative and policy agenda focused on equalizing access; (2) describe the political and budgetary contexts that will frame the way in which these goals are perceived and determine their priority and viability; and (3) explore strategies for, and assess the likelihood of, achieving these goals in light of the political and budgetary constraints identified.

## POLICY PRIORITIES

Having diagnosed "unmet need" as the central, fixable cause of unequal access to higher education, *Access Denied* outlined a straightforward agenda for "renewing the access strategy." According to the report, the following goals are both imperative and achievable:

- First, the nation's longstanding access goal must be reinstated and federal student aid policy refocused on dramatically reducing current levels of unmet need.

- Second, need-based grant aid must be increased for low-income students by reversing the current policy focus on middle-income affordability and merit.

- Third, the Title IV federal student aid programs—their number, structure, and effectiveness—must be reaffirmed as the nation's long-term solution to solving the access problem.

- Fourth, access partnerships between the federal government, states, and institutions must be rebuilt to leverage and target aid on low-income students. (p. 17)

Many might argue that this list is both uninspired and uninspiring. It clings to "access" as the be-all and end-all of federal higher education policy, setting aside the very real problem of affordability for students from middle-class families. It focuses almost exclusively on the classic mechanism for promoting access—grant aid directed at individuals—ignoring the lessons we have learned over the past three decades about the importance of individual aspiration, mentoring, and academic preparation and support in promoting college entrance and achievement among students from disadvantaged backgrounds. It perpetuates the role of the federal government as an infuser of funds into the higher education system, with no corresponding emphasis on institutional accountability, cost control, or measures of value added. Finally, its suggestion that "access partnerships" should be "rebuilt" to coordinate and target aid more effectively on those who need it begs the crucial question of how this coordination, which has persistently eluded us, is to be achieved.

The counterargument, of course, is that the original aim of the Higher Education Act of 1965—to remove financial barriers to higher education—was an important and achievable goal that remains unfulfilled. The federal government does not and should not play a broad, operational role in higher education, and a single-minded focus on ensuring access is an appropriate, enabling role for the federal government at the margin. Furthermore, the structure enacted in the original legislation—a system of portable financial aid composed of grants, loans, and work-study—has been demonstrably effective in promoting access and in supporting a dynamic system of higher education that fosters individual aspiration and institutional diversity. By this view it makes little sense to expand policy goals and diffuse political energy when gains are far more likely to be made through focused advocacy. In short, "the machine ain't broke," and it does not need *fixing*, it needs *funding*.

Both views—and many in between—clearly have some validity, and there is a great deal of room for debate about how the core goals of federal higher education policy should be expanded, reshaped, or rebalanced in preparation for the next reauthorization of the Higher Education Act. Indeed, such debate is already underway. The purpose of this chapter is not to anticipate the outcome of this important debate on policy goals but, rather, to explore the political context against which the debate will play out and to analyze the impact of political and budgetary factors in shaping the goals that may emerge.

## THE POLITICAL CONTEXT

### The Transformed Presidency

On Sunday, September 16, five days after the World Trade Center events, the *New York Times* ran a story on the front page carrying the headline "In Four Days, a National Crisis Changes Bush's Presidency" (Sanger & Van Natta, 2001). The story opened as follows:

> President Bush was sitting in a second grade classroom in Sarasota, Fla., on Tuesday morning, his eyes and his smile fixed on 7-year-olds showing off their reading skills. But his mind was clearly fixed on the news he had heard just moments before: a passenger jet had crashed into one of the World Trade Center towers.
>
> At 9:05 A.M., the White House chief of staff, Andrew H. Card Jr., stepped into the classroom and whispered into the president's right ear, "A second plane hit the other tower, and America's under attack.". . . .
>
> In the course of the next four days, George W. Bush was transformed into a president at the helm of a White House, and a nation, in crisis. (p. 1)

The events described are significant not only because of what happened to redirect President Bush's attention and priorities but also because of where he was sitting when that redirection occurred. Until September 11, President Bush had focused his energies largely on two priorities: tax cuts and education. As of September 11, however, Bush was forced to exit the symbolic—and, some would argue, optional—role of a president concerned with education and assume the mandatory duties of commander in chief of a nation under attack.

## The Education President—Almost

From the day he assumed office, George W. Bush seemed determined to avenge the failed moniker of his father, the putative "education president," whose record on education William Clinton parodied to great advantage as he mapped out the most ambitious federal education agenda in history. "Bipartisan education reform will be the cornerstone of my Administration," wrote President George W. Bush in the forward to the education reform legislation he sent to the Hill on his second day in office (Bush, 2001c). In a speech to the National Urban League delivered at a key moment in the congressional debate over reauthorization of the Elementary and Secondary Education Act in summer 2001, Bush stressed: "Education is a local responsibility; yet improving our schools is a national goal. And all of us must do our part" (Bush, 2001e). More sweeping still: "The progress of our economy and the future of our children starts [sic] in the classroom. And that's why education must be our nation's highest priority" (Bush, 2001d).

Many would argue that even before September 11, education was at best this President Bush's *second* priority—some distance behind the $1.35 trillion tax cut passed on June 7, 2001, as the last major act of a Congress under full Republican control. But without question, education has been an important focus of President Bush's time and attention and political capital.

Bush's first budget, submitted in April, called for increases in the Department of Education budget exceeding those for any federal agency (Bush, 2001b).[2] This was a far cry from the call of former speaker of the House Newt Gingrich, in 1995, to eliminate the Department altogether. And the president spent a great deal of time before September 11 squeezed into tiny little desks in schoolrooms across the country—in St. Louis; Columbus, Ohio; Townsend, Tennessee; and Albuquerque, New Mexico— working to conclude the reauthorization of the Elementary and Secondary Education Act, complete with federally mandated annual tests in grades 3 through 8. Again, a far cry from the once-unrelieved insistence on "local control."

It is not difficult to discern the reasons for this attention. Since 1996 education has ranked consistently as one of the top issues of voter concern

(Bendetto, 1996). In a series of national polls in late August and early September 2001—before the World Trace Center crisis—education was the number one or number two concern, behind only the economy, when it was behind at all (Gallup Organization, 2001; PollingReport.com, 2001). In the early 1970s, at the time of perhaps the most important legislation in the history of higher education policy, only 2 percent of the American public even listed education among issues of national importance (Spencer, 1999).

In considering the newfound prominence of education as a national issue, it is important to note that the focus of public and political concern is overwhelmingly on K–12 education and basic issues of quality in American public schools. Although higher education benefits in important ways from education as a generic priority, for reasons outlined below, higher education priorities also suffer in important ways from the dominance of K–12 concerns.

## The Education Agenda after September 11

It is far too early to assess the extent or durability of September 11's impact on domains of domestic policymaking unrelated to the security environment and immediate economic concerns. Whatever its long-term effects, September 11 reframed in a morning the Bush presidency, and in a profound, even if ultimately short-lived sense, changed the context in which political, legislative, and budget priorities are set at the federal level.

The effects of September 11 were manifest swiftly and decisively in the realm of public opinion. Surveys conducted the week following the attacks found a "total reversal in how much people say they trust the government 'to do what is right'" (McInturff, 2001).[3] Confidence in government reached a thirty-five-year high, returning to levels not seen since the Viet Nam War (McInturff, 2001).

At the same time, public opinion research showed a dramatic drop in consumer confidence beginning shortly after the attack, with a surge of people saying the economy was in recession (McInturff, 2001). This sentiment was later confirmed when the National Bureau of Economic Research (NBER) Business Cycle Dating Committee officially declared the economy in recession on November 26, 2001 (Business Cycle Dating Committee, 2001). The NBER report declared that a peak in business activity occurred in March 2001, marking the end of a cycle of expansion and the beginning of a recession. In short, the events of September 11 appear to have hastened and deepened negative economic trends already in progress.

For education, as for all other domestic policy areas other than security and the economy, these realities mean diminishing priority and shrinking resources. A Fox News poll conducted the week after the attacks asked people an open-ended question about the two most important issues for government to address. The public's response focused overwhelmingly on two issues: terrorism and the economy. The last time an open-ended question was so clearly confined to two issues was in 1982, when, in the wake of double-digit unemployment, Americans focused on unemployment and Social Security as the critical issues.[4] Significantly, however, although education, like health care, Social Security, and Medicare and Medicaid dropped significantly in public concern after September 11, it remains the number one domestic policy issue cited after terrorism and the economy (McInturff, 2001).[5]

## ECONOMIC AND BUDGETARY REALITIES

Notwithstanding education's continued *relative* priority as a political and policy concern, it faces increased competition for significantly shrinking resources. As earlier chapters have detailed, the most important and effective mechanism for promoting access to higher education—financial aid in the form of grants—comes out of the discretionary side of the federal budget. For a long time, the discretionary budget has been under pressure from growing entitlements, and this situation will only grow worse as the nation ages. Thus even in the booming economy of the last decade, we did not see significant growth in discretionary spending on federal financial aid.

More immediate economic trends promise to cause further pressure on domestic discretionary spending. Even before the events of September 11, the stalling economy was beginning to cause a decline in federal revenues, and the $1.35 trillion tax cut passed in June 2001 shrank the pie even further. As has been widely noted, even the whopping price tag of $1.35 trillion significantly understates the actual cost of the tax-cut package. Not-so-subtle budget alchemy was employed to keep the tax package within prescribed budgetary limits.[6] Under the circumstances, it was not altogether surprising when the Congressional Budget Office released revised budget estimates in August 2001, projecting a seriously diminished budget surplus.[7]

In a speech to the National Press Club on November 28, 2001, Mitch Daniels, director of the Office of Management and Budget, underscored the challenges facing the federal budget for the foreseeable future. Noting that "we have, within a very short time, experienced a costly convergence of factors that has led to a dramatic shift in both our near- and long-term fiscal prospects," Daniels provided the following analysis:

> The converging factors are: the recession, the newly necessary spending—imperative spending to deal with the two new threats—the two new needs to defeat terrorism abroad and to defend our homeland. There also have been, coincident with this, new estimates of long-term growth that are somewhat lower than those that all economists, ours, others in the government, and those in the private sector, agreed on just a few short months ago.... And this has profound effects, when compounded out over time on the amount of money that we can expect to have available in the federal treasury. (Daniels, 2001)

Adding these factors together, Daniels noted that it was "regrettably" his conclusion that the federal budget would likely remain in deficit until fiscal year 2005. Daniels went on to stress that these budget constraints would inevitably require difficult tradeoffs. He noted, for example that between 1939 and 1944, domestic spending was cut by 22 percent, and by 37 percent between 1942 and 1944 alone. During the Korean War, non-defense spending dropped in one year, from 1950 to 1951, by one-fourth.

Federal budget pressures mirror and amplify economic forces that are squeezing higher education—both public systems and private institutions—in fundamental ways. The faltering economy has brought a decline in state revenues, which in turn decreases state support for higher education. Each week brings new stories of sharp tuition rises (University of Minnesota, 12 percent; University of Tennessee, 13 percent; Clemson, 25 percent), building projects deferred or suspended, and professorships going unfilled (Steinberg, 2001). As earlier chapters have noted, these economic effects come at a time when the pressures on public systems of higher education, in particular, are large and growing, given significant increases in the number of 18- to 24-year-olds over the next fifteen years.

Private higher education institutions face similar pressures as all revenue sources—endowment returns, gifts, and ability (and willingness) of parents to pay the premium for private higher education—are co-determined by the same economic forces. Thus a downturn in the economy affects the operating budgets of even the best-endowed private colleges and universities in fundamental ways. These institutions, like their public counterparts, will face serious pressure to raise tuition.

Because the political system, reflecting public opinion, is deeply skeptical about the cost of higher education, the net result of rising tuition is to render higher education politically more suspect at precisely the time that competition for domestic federal resources will be significantly more intense (Spencer, 1999). In other words, as parents, students, and institutions need more government support to compensate for shrinking private resources, federal politicians and policymakers are likely to be preoccupied with issues of cost, rather than financial aid.

## HIGHER EDUCATION IN A K–12 WORLD

Higher education faces competition not only from domestic priorities other than education but also from the emphasis within the domain of education on the K–12 agenda. Note where President Bush was to be found when he learned of the World Trade Tower calamity. Not in the White House, ready to be hustled to the Situation Room, but parked in a second grade classroom in Sarasota Florida, endeavoring to increase pressure for passage of the reauthorization of the Elementary and Secondary Education Act, then bottled up in a contentious House and Senate conference committee.

To be sure, higher education has enjoyed a certain "coattail effect" from the public preoccupation with the problems facing our schools. Although it is K–12 issues that have overwhelmingly driven public concern, because "education" has achieved sacred cow status, politicians have been loathe to cut education funding at any level. Thus, as outlined in earlier chapters, traditional higher education programs have been protected and enjoyed moderate increases since 1995, and the Pell program has received substantial increases. Even though the significant new money for higher education has been directed to tax benefits (the Hope Scholarship and Lifelong Learning Tax Credits in the Taxpayer Relief Act of 1997), these new funds have been accompanied by increases in traditional student aid programs as well (see Chapter 5).

### The Attention Problem

Although higher education has been a collateral beneficiary of strong public concern with the state of our nation's public school systems, the overwhelming emphasis on K–12 issues has serious implications for higher education. The secretary of education is a former school superintendent, and the position of assistant secretary for postsecondary education remained unfilled well into Bush's first year (Paige, 2001). Notwithstanding significant rhetorical attention to the Pell grant program, President Bush's first budget request called for a mere $100 increase in the maximum grant. Several other core student aid programs—work-study, Supplemental Educational Opportunity Grants (SEOG), Perkins Loans, and Leveraging Educational Assistance Partnerships (LEAP)—received no additional monies at all under the Bush plan (Association of American Universities, 2002). Congress increased funding for LEAP, SEOG and Perkins Loans, but work-study received no additional money (Association of American Universities, 2002).

People talk about the "attention" economy—namely, that with today's overload of information in all media it is difficult for any given message or product to get through the noise to claim the attention of a given customer. Higher education faces similar obstacles in the political economy. A Senate Democratic press conference in early August, the day after President Bush gave an important speech addressing issues in the then-pending elementary and secondary legislation, illustrates the point:

QUESTION: Senator Daschle, there's been a lot of talk that, with the President's education package, there still isn't time for higher education legislation. Do you see any time this session to take anything up on the floor?

SEN. DASCHLE: Well, I would defer to Senator Dodd. He has been one of *the* experts on education, and let me ask for his comment on that.

SEN. DODD: Well, we've made good progress on the Elementary and Secondary Education Act in the conference. Yesterday, in fact, a number of provisions were resolved between the House and the Senate, and the committee staffs are going to work the entire month of August on some of the thornier questions between the two bills....

But I'd be more optimistic about having some time to consider higher education issues in that we're not looking at the kind—at least the mood of the conference yesterday was extremely upbeat and extremely positive and extremely cooperative. The president's speech yesterday [on the Elementary and Secondary Act] before the Urban League was a very positive statement, I think, on accountability standards [in K–12], the testing and so forth, looking—to paraphrase his line, it's not to set tests or standards that are so high that no one can pass them—we saw as a very welcome indication. His remarks that he knows there's no real need for increased spending in this area [e.g., K–12 testing] were very constructive statements to make in those remarks.

QUESTION: So there's still a good likelihood of higher education as well?

SEN. DODD: Hm?

QUESTION: So there still is a good likelihood of higher education legislation as well?

SEN. DODD: Well, I don't want to—obviously, Senator Kennedy would be the person to talk directly about that.... (Federal News Service, 2001)

## The Problem of Leakage

Even when higher education succeeds in getting the attention of the public and policymakers, it risks not getting the type of attention it needs.

As illustrated by the rather amusing exchange above, the same political leaders responsible for our federal higher education policy are preoccupied with K–12 concerns, creating not only the problem of attention, but also of carry-over. The policy concerns in elementary and secondary education—quality and accountability—are emphatically not those that have historically animated federal higher education policy.

In the domain of higher education, the federal government has for the last half-century defined its role in narrow, instrumental terms at the margin, leaving operating responsibility and issues of curriculum and quality to states and private boards of trustees. Until the 1990s (when we adopted large-scale tax measures directed at education), we chose to fund individual students through mechanisms that rely on higher education professionals—namely, financial aid officers—to construct financial aid packages that take into account the economic circumstances of each individual student and his or her family, as well as the specific cost structure of the institution student has chosen to attend. These judgments trigger the flow of federal funds because a given student's access to various types of grants and loans—Supplemental Educational Opportunity Grants, Perkins loans, work-study, and so on—depends on the relationship between eligibility criteria at the federal level and costs, packaging practices, and availability of various funds at the institutional level. Thus federal financial aid funds enter the higher education system in a mechanistic fashion, with important value judgments, such as the kind of education sought by a given individual and the curriculum and cost structure mounted by a given institution, left to other actors.

The federal role in K–12 education is quite different. Public schooling has historically been quintessentially the subject of "local control." As the problems with public education have intruded ever more insistently into public consciousness, however, federal policymakers have abandoned their reticence about inserting themselves in this domain. When they do, they concern themselves not with cost and access, but with issues that go to the core of the educational experience—the quality of instruction and the academic progress of students.

For large segments of the population, our public school system has failed in its basic educational mission. President Bush expressed the problem as follows in the "No Child Left Behind" legislation he sent to the Hill on his second weekday in office:

Today, nearly 70 percent of inner city fourth graders are unable to read at a basic level on national reading tests. Our high school seniors trail students in Cyprus and South Africa on international math tests. And nearly a third of our college freshman find they must take a remedial course before they are able to even begin regular college level courses.

Although education is primarily a state and local responsibility, the federal government is partly at fault for tolerating these abysmal results. The federal government currently does not do enough to reward success and sanction failure in our education system (Bush, 2001c, p. 2).

Bush's characterization of the problem doubtless has merit. But in public education, as in our war against terrorism, the enemy is difficult to identify and the federal response, in particular, is thus difficult to fashion. The resulting policy is often diffuse and comprised more of symbolism and bluster than coherent policy content.

Because the federal government does not, in fact, have its hands on the reigns of the K–12 educational enterprise, a fundamental problem that goes to the essence of how teachers teach and students learn is dealt with, in federal policymaking, in the language of accountability. What we cannot fix, we can at least *count* or measure. President Bush again:

> For nearly forty years, our federal government has tried to improve education with money alone. We invested $158 billion in Title I programs, with great intentions and no measurable result. We've been pumping gas into a flooded engine. Just as faith with out works is dead, money without reform is fruitless.
>
> Yet, today, after decades of frustration, we're on the verge of dramatic reform. Schools must have the resources they need, and I support more spending. Local folks must be in charge of local schools, because they're closest to the children and their challenges. But most of all, we need true accountability, the centerpiece of reform. Consequences for school officials must be determined by proven results for children. Those in authority must show responsibility. The purpose of education is, after all, not jobs for adults, it's learning for students (Bush, 2001e).

Embodying this focus on accountability, the president asked Congress to pass legislation that would provide for, among other things, annual testing in reading and math in grades 3 through 8 and funding correlated to performance on the tests. Under the president's plan, federal funds would reward states and schools that improve achievement, and certain funds would be withdrawn from states that permit student performance to decline (Bush, 2001a).

For higher education the implications of this kind of approach are potentially significant. In a domain characterized historically by circumspection and restraint, federal policymakers seem content to reach into the heart of the enterprise, insist on objective measures to judge student achievement and progress, and use federal funds to reward and punish based on these measures.

## POLICY IMPLICATIONS

Teasing out the implications of these broad contextual factors for specific policy agendas is inevitably a speculative exercise, made more so by the fact that, as noted above, we do not have broad agreement on the way higher education's core policy goals should be framed going forward. In order to anchor the analysis, however, I will return to the goals outlined in the *Access Denied* report. Again, the claim is not that these goals are comprehensive. Rather, they are simple and straightforward and offer a coherent approach to at least one central goal of higher education policy— namely, promoting equal access. Precisely because of their simplicity, they provide a convenient means for analyzing the effects on policy of the political and budgetary factors outlined above.

As outlined in *Access Denied*, in practical terms reviving the access agenda means first, restoring a genuine and substantive—as distinct from a purely rhetorical—commitment to fostering access as the core concern of federal higher education policy. Second, it means increasing funding from the federal discretionary budget for outright need-based grants. Third, it means aligning federal, state, and institutional initiatives so they are not working at cross purposes and the funds, once they reach the student from whatever source, are effectively targeted to close the gap between educational expenses and financial aid. Although *Access Denied* expresses a fourth goal—maintaining the number and structure of current federal student aid programs—I would argue that a precise commitment to the structure of current programs is not, strictly speaking, necessary if goals one and two—actually renewing the commitment to access and increasing grant funding—were achieved.

### Restoring the Commitment to Access

The inexorable shift in the 1980s and 1990s away from the goal of access for low-income students to the middle-class concern for affordability can be traced to a number of interacting causes: first, the preoccupation of the political process with polling and public opinion, made possible—many would argue inevitable—by the rapid advances in the technologies that allow us to gauge and manipulate public opinion; second, the increasing dependence of politicians on money to win elections precisely because of these technologies and their expense; third, the steady rise in the economic returns to higher education and the corresponding decline in the value of a high school degree, transforming higher education, in the mind of the broad public, from a luxury to a necessity; and, fourth, the aggressive above-inflation increases in the price of tuition throughout the 1980s and into the mid-1990s, causing this necessity to seem, for many, unaffordable.

In other words, politicians, increasingly dependent on broad support to win elections, emphasized the programs that would appeal to middle-class voters. In that way, the political domain has, over the last twenty years, come increasingly to mirror as well as amplify values and rewards present in the marketplace. By contrast, when Lyndon Johnson signed the Higher Education Act of 1965, it was part of the War on Poverty, the higher education component of his Great Society program that viewed government as a means to compensate for the failures of the market (Spencer, 1999). Johnson assumed that students from middle-class families could go to college if they so chose. His goal was to ensure that "a high school student anywhere in this great land of ours can apply to any college or any university in any of the fifty states and not be turned away because his family is poor" (Johnson, 1965, p. 1102).

In the aftermath of September 11 and its impact on an already faltering economy, one could argue that at the level of public values, there is scant hope for a recommitment to the access agenda. Middle-class parents, perpetually anxious about the cost of college, can only be expected to become more so as their own economic circumstances worsen and tuitions once again rise sharply. Yet, as noted above, the events of September 11 had an immediate (though one does not yet know how durable) effect on the view of the public toward government. For the first time since the early Johnson years, confidence in government has risen dramatically, and the public seems to see for it a role distinct from that of the private sector—witness the federalizing of airport security. Add to this the post–September 11 outpouring of support for public service and community values (again one does not know how durable these sentiments are), and there is some reason for optimism that policymakers and the public may begin to think in a more disciplined and other-directed way about the role government should play across a broad range of areas.

## Increasing Grant Funding

This piece of reviving the access agenda will be enormously difficult, yet without it the other goals are more or less paper tigers. As noted above, the pressures on domestic discretionary spending, already large and growing because of demographic forces and entitlement obligations set in motion long ago, have increased dramatically, at least in the short term, because of the economic downturn and spending requirements to meet military and security needs. Arguably, the main source of optimism in this area is precisely the starkness of the tradeoffs that will have to be made across the federal budget. If, as suggested above, progress is made in articulating the importance of the access goal with clarity and focus, traditional financial aid programs may compete relatively better for scarce resources than for a portion of larger, more diffuse expenditures.

More realistically, student loans, which are built into the mandatory budget, and tax measures, which once enacted are difficult to repeal, have an enormous budgetary advantage over grant funding, which must be allocated each year. Furthermore, higher education grant programs will, as noted above, have difficulty competing with K–12 initiatives, which are also funded from the discretionary budget. This most crucial piece of the access agenda is thus without doubt very fragile indeed.

## Better Coordination and Targeting

More effective coordination and targeting of need-based aid assumes that funds from federal, state, and institutional sources would be administered such that for a given academically prepared student, financial needs are not overmet or undermet. It suggests that we would spend less public and institutional money on merit aid not tied to need. And it would mean that we pay attention to students early enough in the educational pipeline to increase the number of students served and the likelihood that a given student will persist with his or her education through high school and completion of a college degree.

As the discussion in the foregoing chapters emphasizes, however, we are currently on a path away from, rather than toward, more targeted and coordinated aid. Achieving greater coordination among aid at different levels would in some cases require significant policy and programmatic shifts that are not likely to be undertaken in the absence of a secure funding environment. At the federal level, for example, eligibility criteria within the Pell Grant program make even trivial increases in the maximum grant level enormously expensive because the formula that increases the maximum also expands the population eligible for minimum grants. Furthermore, since the Pell program was designed and funded primarily with the needs of traditional college-age students in mind, at current funding levels it has increasing difficulty keeping pace with the differential need structures of dependent and independent students. Yet modifying the Pell program to address either of those issues—for example, by creating separate grant programs for dependent and independent students—would risk cutting one group out of funding altogether in the current budgetary environment.

At the institutional level, since non-need-based aid is a key component of institutional competitiveness and, in certain cases, survival, better leveraging of need-based aid will, as suggested in Chapter 5, require collective action among institutions or the targeting of certain types of government aid toward institutions that adopt particular need-based policies. Since either of these strategies may have the effect of differentiating among classes of institutions based on wealth (e.g., privileging wealthier institutions), they would need to be thought through very carefully. At the state level, as pointed out in Chapter 4, it is not difficult from a policy point of view to link eligibility for merit aid to a demonstration of need, as the CalGrant program has recently done. Nonetheless, broad merit programs like the Georgia HOPE Scholarship remain enormously popular and have been adopted by a number of different states. Once such benefits are in place, they are very difficult to take away.

The challenges of coordinating existing sources of aid are made all the more difficult by the K–12 "leakage" problem discussed above. The emphasis on student achievement and accountability that have emerged as proxies for addressing issues of quality in the public schools may threaten the federal approach to student aid at precisely the time it needs to be focused and strengthened.

First, preoccupation with K–12 concerns may place undue legislative and funding emphasis on teacher training, mentoring and academic preparation, and remediation, for example—areas directly and concretely linked to the quality of the K–12 education system. Although these are doubtless areas worthy of concern and policy development, they are not necessarily those higher education would place at the top of a priority list in an environment of scarce resources.

Second, the focus on student achievement may increase rather than decrease the relative growth of merit-based aid. In the K–12 environment, student achievement typically refers to the academic progress of cohorts of students, and it is used as a measure of, and proxy for, the quality of the educational experience. In the student aid environment, however, which has at its best historically been driven by the talents and aspirations of individual students, academic achievement is easily conflated with individual performance or merit.

Third, the preoccupation with measuring outcomes may result in tying federal student aid to individual and institutional outcomes (such as graduation rates), thus, for example, penalizing dropouts and institutions that serve the most difficult populations, rather than directing resources to strengthen the pipeline on the front end. Finally, the preoccupation with accountability will almost surely increase the federal attention to college cost and tuition rates precisely when both public and private institutions face maximum economic pressure and constrained revenue sources.

In short, although the benefits of greater targeting and coordination are manifest, the impediments to undertaking the integrated policy review that such coordination presupposes are significant. The best hope, again, is that a highly constrained funding environment will introduce discipline that is not likely to come from elsewhere.

## CONCLUSION

The Higher Education Act of 1965 was signed into law at a time when government was understood to have a clear and important role to play. The policy objectives of the legislation were few, its instrumentalities were clean, its partnerships and pipeline mechanisms straightforward. Now, four decades later, we have new evidence showing we are still a distance from achieving the act's core objective of promoting equality of access to higher education. But we also have evidence that this objective can be served, at least in part, in a simple and straightforward way by directing money to academically prepared students who have unmet financial need.

The events of September 11 have caused our society and economy to slow down, quite literally. In some ways—like the interruption of our transportation and postal systems—the slowdown has been highly disruptive. Yet it has also caused individuals and communities, for the moment, at least, to clarify values and pursue common objectives with focus and courage. Thanks to the research and analysis reflected in the foregoing chapters, we have a clear picture of what works and what does not work to assure that academically prepared students may attend college regardless of their financial circumstances. Now, perhaps, we can renew the access agenda with focus and commitment.

## NOTES

This chapter is based in part on a paper delivered as part of the 2000 Symposium of the Forum for the Future of Higher Education, published in *Forum Futures, 2002*. The views expressed in this chapter are those of the author and do not reflect any position by or on behalf of Harvard University.

1. The Hope Scholarship and Lifetime Learning Tax Credits took effect in 1998, and are expected to cost the federal government $12–$15 billion in lost rev-

enues annually once the law is fully phased in by fiscal year 2002. By contrast, federal grant programs provided under $9 billion per year as of 2000 (College Board, 2001; Office of Management and Budget, 2001).

2. Bush's budget called for an increase of 11%, to $44.5 billion, for the Department of Education's budget.

3. Citing *Washington Post*, 2/26/1985–9/27/2001/Michigan-American National Election Study, 1958–1982. This survey shows that since the early 1970s the number of people who trusted government to do what was right always, most of the time, or some of the time was never more than 48%—a mark it hit in the Reagan years—but throughout the 1990s never exceeded 34%. In surveys following September 11, the percent nearly doubled, to 64%.

4. Fox News Poll, 9/19–20/01, cited in McInturff (2001).

5. In March, 2001, 29% of those surveyed said that education was one of the two most important issues for government to address. On September 19–20, that proportion had fallen to 12%, twice that of the next highest domestic concern—family values at 6%.

6. Most of the tax cuts are phased in very slowly; the estate tax repeal, for example, is not fully phased in until 2010, with all the provisions sunset by 2011, and some in 2010, even though it would be an unusual Congress that failed to extend popular tax provisions. Finally, the legislation left out altogether major tax cut measures—such as the extension of the Research and Experimentation tax credit—that are virtually certain to be enacted in the near future.

7. The Congressional Budget Office's revised forecasts, issued on August 28, 2001, projected a surplus of $49 billion between 2002 and 2006—a mere 5% of the $987 billion predicted in the January (2001) baseline (Crippen, 2001, January and August).

## REFERENCES

Advisory Committee on Student Financial Assistance. (2001). *Access denied: Restoring the nation's commitment to equal educational opportunity.* Washington, DC: Author.

Association of American Universities. (2002, January 9). Fiscal year 2002 Labor-HHS appropriations. (http://www.aau.edu/budget/2002LHHSEdTable .html). Washington, DC: Author.

Bendetto, R. (1996, January 10). Keys to '96 campaign. *USA Today*, p. A1.

Bush, G. W. (2001a). A blueprint for new beginnings: A responsible budget for America's priorities. The president's FY02 budget submission to Congress, February. (http://www.whitehouse.gov/new/usbudget/blueprint/budtoc .html). Washington, DC: Office of the President.

Bush, G. W. (2001b). The budget message of the president. April 9, 2001. Message submitted to Congress with budget. (http://www.whitehouse.gov /omb/budget /fy2002/budi.html). Washington, DC: Office of the President.

Bush, G. W. (2001c). No child left behind. Elementary and Secondary bill submitted by President to Congress. (http://www.whitehouse.gov/news/reports/no-child-left-behind.html). Washington, DC: Office of the President.

Bush, G. W. (2001d). Radio address by the president to the nation, September 1. Washington, DC: Office of the President.

Bush, G. W. (2001e). Remarks to the 2001 National Urban League Conference, August 1. Washington, DC. (http://www.whitehouse.gov/news/releases/2001/08/20010801-3.html). Washington, DC: Office of the President.

Business Cycle Dating Committee. (2001). Report: The business-cycle peak of March 2001, November 26. (http://www.nber.org/cycles/november2001/). Cambridge, MA: National Bureau of Economic Research.

College Board. (2001). *Trends in student aid*. New York: Author.

Crippen, D. (2001, January). The budget and economic outlook: Fiscal years 2002–2011. (http://www.cbo.gov/showdoc.cfm?index=2727&sequence=0). Washington, DC: Congressional Budget Office.

Crippen, D. (2001, August). The budget and economic outlook: An update. (http://www.cbo.gov/showdoc.cfm?index=3019&sequence=0&from=7). Washington, DC: Congressional Budget Office.

Daniels, M. (2001). Mitch Daniels delivers remarks to the National Press Club, November 28. (http://www.whitehouse.gov/omb/pubpress/2001-61.html). Washington, DC: Office of Management and Budget.

Federal News Service. (2001, August 2). Regular media availability with Senate Majority Leader Thomas Daschle (D-SD). Also participating: Senator Christopher Dodd (D-CT). Senate Democratic Leadership Press Conference. The Capitol, S-224, Washington, DC.

Gallup Organization. (2001). Most important problem. (http://www.gallup.com/poll/indicators/indmip.asp). Princeton, NJ: Author.

Johnson, L. B. (1965). Remarks at Southwest Texas State College upon signing the Higher Education Act of 1965, November 8. Public Papers of the Presidents 602: 1102.

McInturff, W. D. (2001, October 9). American post attack: Observations about recent national survey data. (www.pos.org/presentations/two.ppt). Alexandria, VA: Public Opinion Strategies.

Office of Management and Budget. (2001). Tax expenditures by function. (http://www.whitehouse.gov/omb/budget/fy2002/bud22_4.html). Washington, DC: Author.

Paige, R. (2001, December 5). Press release: Bryant named deputy assistant for postsecondary education. (http://www.ed.gov/PressReleases/12-2001/12052001.html). Washington, DC: Department of Education.

PollingReport.com. (2001). Problems and priorities. CBS News Poll. August 28–31, 2001. Harris Poll. August 15–22, 2001. ABC News/Washington Post Poll. March 22–25, 2001 and September 4–6, 2000. Newsweek Poll. December 14–15, 2000. Business Week/Harris Poll. July 21–23, 2000. (http://www.pollingreport.com/prioriti.htm).

Sanger, D. E, & Van Natta, Jr., D. (2001, September 16). After the attacks: The events; in four days, a national crisis changes Bush's presidency. *New York Times*, p. 1.

Spencer, A.C. (1999). The new politics of education. In J.E. King (ed.), *Financing a college education: How it works, how it's changing*. Phoenix, AZ: Oryx Press.

Steinberg, J. (2001, September 7). State colleges, feeling pinch, cut costs and raise tuitions. *New York Times*, p. A1.

# Index